Decolonizing Awareness:
Convergence in history

Eva Maria Portillo

Published by Mariposa Books
Toronto, Canada

© Eva Maria Portillo 2016

ISBN: 978-0-9952443-0-6

Cover and Images by Eva Maria Portillo

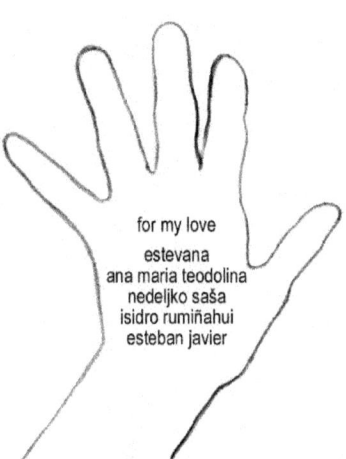

Decolonizing Awareness: Convergence in History

PART ONE: HISTORY 'AS PAST'   1

PART TWO: DOMINANT HISTORY   7

    Chapter One: The realist paradigm   15

PART THREE: HISTORY DISCIPLINED   33

    Chapter Two: From materialism to iteration   37

    Chapter Three: Critical historiography   64

PART FOUR: ITERATIONS OF HISTORY   77

    Chapter Four: A critical precedent   81

    Chapter Five: Technologies of empire   93

PART FIVE: PERCEIVING CONVERGENCE   113

Works Cited   139

PART ONE:
History 'as past'

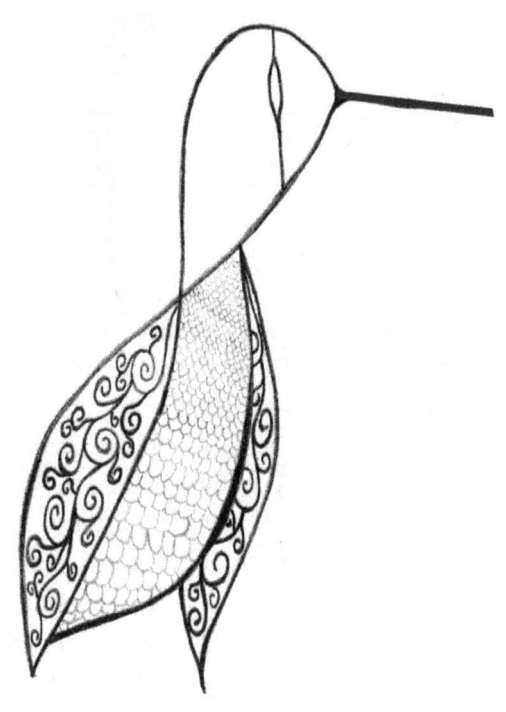

This book is about historical awareness. Historical awareness as being able to perceive what has been, what is. The central premise of this book is that being aware of history is to experience history intimately. When history is studied in the university, without feeling and relying on facts, historical awareness is colonized. To decolonize this awareness is to perceive convergence in history.

I could only respect my understanding of colonialism once I acknowledged my awareness of history. What I perceived to be true went against what I was taught to be true. In listening to myself I did not ignore what I was taught, but rather, sought to understand why I had been taught the way that I had been. The way I was taught history, and what constituted history, was deliberately different from my awareness. It is not a coincidence that the lived experiences of colonialism do not readily emerge from within disciplined history.

The problem is that we do not perceive colonialism. We know about it. We know about it as something beyond the body. To know something beyond the body is critically different from experiencing perception from within the body. To know is to engage knowledge as an externality. To perceive is to experience reality intimately. To perceive is to feel, experience, interpolate, sense, and relate to reality. In perception, reality is intimate. For the most part, the intimacy of perceptible reality is withheld from us, as we are taught that knowledge is not of the body. As a result of this teaching we do not perceive reality and are content to know facts. Because we believe that knowledge is not of the body we do not experience knowledge intimately. As a consequence, we become unaware of perceptible reality. To be in a state of unawareness is a process that restricts understanding of the totality of the current social situation.

Awareness is being in reality. When knowledge is structured so is our awareness. We perceive along the lines of how our awareness is structured. When knowledge is structured in the university we perceive in accordance to the realist paradigm. Historical knowledge is taught according to the realist paradigm, based on reading textbooks that contain names, dates, places, events and so forth. The study of history is based on those textbooks, paying particular attention to the facts: the when, where, who, what and why of events. In the way history is taught, its intimacy becomes illusive. Historical awareness is encountered as an external experience, and only accessible by way of experts. Intimate awareness of history becomes difficult to experience when history is thought to be an externality of facts and narratives. In this way, historical knowledge becomes structured by practices of the discipline. Historical perception is altered according to the way that historical knowledge has been structured. It is altered to experience history as a impersonal passive externality. The university has colonized history by creating disciplinary methods that structure historical awareness to deny history as an experience of intimate perception.

Historical knowledge in the university is based on the dominant narrative of its development as a European institution. The methods of the discipline of history oversee research to solidify realist principles. History, based on the realist paradigm, is predisposed to disavow colonialism. The disavowal of colonialism is facilitated by the erasure of dynamic movement and time. History in the context of the university has been created in such a way that the dynamic global processes of Empire and colonialism cannot be studied by the methods and practices of the discipline. Since historical knowledge of the university is misrepresented, and its relation to colonialism disavowed, awareness of the totality of colonialism becomes illusive. Decolonization includes developing a communal understanding of the problem; the problem of colonialism. A process facilitated by creating a vision/ing of colonialism. Decolonization includes reaching conceptual convergence in the analysis of colonialism and creating a movement away from the realist paradigm.

The illusion of objective history based on facts has been made possible by a belief in realism. The realist paradigm in the university has created an institutional focus on the production of specialized knowledge. Specialized knowledge is produced in the university by disciplinary experts; experts writing an exposition of detailed facts. Resulting in a situation where experts become so specialized in their fields that they cannot have a conversation about their work outside of their field of study. This is a relatively new phenomenon in learning. According to Einstein (2007), to be educated meant having a breadth of knowledge that was multi-disciplinary; this included having an understanding of the sciences, mathematics, arts, humanities, and philosophy (xiii). This is a very different understanding of education that we now have in the university. To be an educated person now means to be an expert, to gain specialized knowledge in one discipline. This is a concerning development in the state of knowledge. This aesthetic of specialization is based on a preference for the specific. In a feverish rush to theorize the particular and singular the whole and general are being disregarding. Leading to an aesthetic commitment where social theorists are less concerned with accounting for reality and more focused on detailing small-scale phenomena.

In this way, history has been disciplined. It has followed the path of knowledge production based on conquest, plunder and has actively participated in silencing that reality. The discipline of history has established itself by assuming that there is a past waiting to be made into a narrative, and the work of the historian is to collect facts about the past and write narratives. The discipline has developed in such a way that its methods obscure key elements about how human beings are regulated and subjected to violence. A decolonizing historiography focuses on key elements traditionally obscured by dominant historiography. Specifically, a decolonizing historiography seeks to understand the role colonialism in the development of the discipline of history. Moreover, decolonizing historiography looks to name the ways in which the university is implicated in the colonization of our historical awareness.

A component of a decolonizing historiography traces the university's role in colonialism. In particular, a decolonizing historiography begins with the premise that the way in which colonialism is defined and researched in the discipline of history produces the erasure and disavowal of colonial relations of the appropriation of knowledge and biocolonialism, for example. Moreover, the way colonialism is defined and researched makes nearly invisible how the appropriation of knowledge and biocolonialism produced technologies of an international infrastructure of imperial states. Technologies used to continue to colonize territories of Empire, both within Europe and beyond.

A central intention of a decolonizing history puts back together the pieces of our collective history that the discipline of history has shattered; a shattering that has served to disappear the role of the university in colonialism, conquest and plunder. In the discipline of history colonialism is narrated as a series of divergent histories that focus on different spaces, temporalities, conceptualizations, definitions, and social actors. Each history is narrated in such a way as to suggest that each history is complete on its own. The historian rarely signals that these histories are dependent on one another for meaning and faithfulness to reality. A critical historian, or communal storyteller, would focus on creating convergent narratives of what has been constructed as divergent.

A key element for decolonizing historiography attempts, whenever possible, to converge historical narratives. In other words, decolonizing history moves away from creating divergent historical narratives by trying to understand how these narratives are connected. As human beings, they are very few of us who have not lived the reality of colonialism, of capitalism, of patriarchy. Therefore, our histories should speak to that truth if we are going to move forward, if we are to grieve, and to heal. This is particularly necessary in the field of history because, as Daniel Fulda (2010) argues, the "historicist mode of thinking about history can shape one's perceptions and experiences" (140). Our belief in the idea of history- the idea that the past created the present and the present will in turn create the future- becomes the basis from which we perceive and experience reality. Using history to understand the

present is a common experience in shaping reality. Thinking historically is
> a habitualised interpretive pattern which categorically accesses, structures and interprets the world... Historicism here is nothing less than a life-conditioning force which is of importance for identity formation; and we are confronted with a model of history which appears so 'alive' that it can actively shape people's lives (Fulda 141).

We interpret the world based on the idea of history; this idea conditions our lives. When historical narratives are based on the logic of separation, and produce divergent narrative, we behave in the world accordingly. History structures our isolation: personally, socially, and our species consciousness.

Moreover, history often narrates the past based on dualistic thinking, what bell hooks names as dominator thinking. For bell hooks (2013),
> [d]ualistic thinking, which is at the core of dominator thinking, teaches people that there is always the oppressed and the oppressor, a victim and a victimizer. Hence there is always someone to blame. Moving past the ideology of blame to a politics of accountability is a difficult move to make in a society where almost all political organizing, whether conservative or radical, has been structures around the binary of good guys and bad guys ... Accountability is more expansive concept because it opens a filed of possibility wherein we are all compelled to move beyond blame to see where our responsibility lies (30).

Dualistic thinking creates definite divergence, colonizer\colonized, Europe\not-Europe, bourgeoisie\proletariats, and so forth. It rarely speaks of the ways in which our experiences and histories are intertwined, which forecloses our ability to understand how our lives and our futures are bound together. Historiography offers a unique opportunity, if we commit to narrating our convergent histories, we may be able to achieve convergence in this moment.

PART TWO:
Dominant history

Colonialism has been described, yet not defined. While there is an abundance of knowledge about colonialism, there is no consensus as to an exact meaning of the word. The practices of colonialism have been documented with respect to the circulation of material wealth and ideologies. However, a precise definition of colonialism is illusive as it has not been significantly theorized as a process. The study of colonialism tends to analyze the terminal points of coloniality, the inception of colonialism and projects established by colonial rule. What is not analyzed is the conditions of possibility for the emergence of colonial projects and their continuity. Culminating into a situation where social theorists, historians and philosophers create divergent accounts of colonialism. The existence of a great deal of divergent understandings of colonialism forecloses the possibility of reaching conceptual convergence. Without conceptual convergence- an agreement of what colonialism is- there can be no significant movement towards a politics or practice of decolonization.

The problem is that colonialism is being analyzed from within a realist paradigm. Within this paradigm the study of reality becomes the study of matter in relation to the natural progression of time- understood as the linear development of time. A realist paradigm is one which establishes reality as that which is tangible, material. It suggests that only quantifiable facts can emerge as representative of reality. It structures what is acceptable knowledge about reality. As a consequence, in the realist paradigm, dynamic motion of energy and time are eclipsed. The totality of a social situation becomes illusive when only minute facts can be spoken. The eclipsing of social reality happens because facts cannot contain dynamic movement, facts can only attest to simply and reducible elements of reality. The totality of dynamic motion, of the complexity of interactions and movement, is disavowed when reality is spoken of only from within a realist paradigm. The erasure of dynamic motion leads to a partial understanding of colonialism. What is disavowed in the realist paradigm is the systematic motion of colonialism. The motion of colonialism is the motion of iteration. Colonialism as an iterative process is an echo. The iterative motion is the repetition of a process intended to create an unbounded sequence of iterations. One iteration is the result of previous iterations. As it travels, colonialism echoes, it reverberates as it conditions. As such the study of a particular iteration provides insight into the system as a whole. As a paradigm, realism does not foreclose a study of colonialism. It does however, structure the study of colonialism in such a way that we have accumulated a lot of data about the inception of colonialism and its projects, which is of limited relevance in the process of decolonization. In the study of colonialism the realist paradigm becomes problematic in the pursuit of conceptual convergence.

When social theorists favour the local and specific, they tend to assert that the most truthful evidence is to be found in tangible facts. However, what many scholars do not fully recognize is that the search for the specific and local is a mobilization of the realist paradigm rooted in classical (outdated) sciences. In the realist paradigm, matter- as theorized by the classical sciences- is understood as the reason for everything. In this paradigm human beings are the sum total of their bodies and the earth consists of a series of interconnected natural phenomena (weather, nutrient cycles, and life cycles). In other words, the realist paradigm gives priority to localized matter;

> The philosophy of realism holds that the fundamental elements of reality are independent of consciousness- this is the doctrine of *strong objectivity* delineated by the Greek philosopher Aristotle, by and large regarded as the father of realism in the West. A tree in the forest is assumed to be real, as is the sound when the tree falls, even though neither may be perceived; the moon continues in its space-time orbit even when no one is looking, and so forth. The doctrine of strong objectivity is augmented by another doctrine, causal determinism- this one bolstered by Newtonian classical physics- according to which all phenomena are causal and determined. There are many different subphilosophies within this basic realist view, and I will mention only the currently dominant one- material or physical realm, which considers

matter (generalized to include energy and fields) to be the only fundamental reality. This is the legacy of another ancient Greek philosopher, namely Democritus. Material realism also holds that there is only one order of reality, matter (and its extensions, energy, and fields); all else, including consciousness, are epiphenomena and are ultimately reducible to matter (Goswami 1993, 187).

Within the realist paradigm it is the development of matter according to causal determinism that is the sum total of reality. This reduces the function and ability of consciousness to matter. In this way, the realist paradigm posits reality as fixed where matter and causality are given analytic priority. This tenet has been taken up by many disciplines and many theories and philosophies, which have been elaborated to sustain the idea that matter and the local are of primary importance.

The need to be specific is a theoretical outcome of adopting a realist paradigm in the analysis of social relations. Often, this focus on the local and specific is defined as desirable and no significant reason given for this desirability: it is assumed to be self-evident. As Goswami (1993) argues,

> materialism comes hand in hand with epiphenomenalism and reductionism. And because there is only one reality, defined by space-time, the doctrine of locality is held to be fundamental. This is the idea that all interactions are local, transmitted via signals through space-time (187).

Critical theory is swayed to an analysis of the local and specific. There exists a lure to theorize the real, the tangible, quantifiable facts from which a general consensus can be reached. An important implication of the realist paradigm is the centrality of the specific and local in the development of critical theory. This perspective privileges the ideas of cause and effect relationships and materiality.

For Goswami (1993), the tenets of the realist paradigm are adopted by many schools of thought- including critical social theory. It is problematic in that the realist paradigm denies dynamic awareness of reality. In contrast to the realist paradigm, quantum modality is based on the idea that consciousness is the basis of reality. In the paradigm of quantum modality, the search for the specific and the local is not an accurate way to account for reality. Quantum modality moves away from the idea that matter is the basis of reality; emphasizing the unity of all consciousness and life, as opposed to the centrality of localized matter. Quantum modality and current developments of the natural sciences in general, pose a challenge to critical theory. Given that critical theory has emerged from a scientific paradigm of realism, how do social theorists take into account developments in the natural sciences, and quantum physics in particular? In other words, if critical theory derives its rationale, or at the very least, its research parameters from a scientific understanding of reality that is problematic, or outdated, then what is the role of the social scientists in evaluating and developing critical theory?

The realist paradigm has been institutionalized as the logic of the university. Teaching and learning have developed to emphasize study of the particular and specific, resulting in the development of divergent narratives. Because the emphasis is on the development of matter, events are described in their contextual uniqueness, evading how events and spaces interact dynamically. Interactions that are irreducible to matter, the specific or linear time become simplified as facts in local space. Research and analysis become divergent when the focus is on contextual specificity, resulting in conceptual divergence in the analysis of colonialism.

The realist paradigm as adopted by the discipline of history poses particular difficulties. The development of historiography within the realist paradigm has led to the disciplinary focus on archival research. Archives are preferred historical data as they are tangible matter available for the historian to scrutinize in the present. Reliance of archival material is institutionally constructed as the pursuit of objectivity in historical writing. The privileging of material artifacts is giving priority to the analysis of matter, thereby subsuming the centrality of historical consciousness and awareness. For the critical historian it becomes necessary to deconstruct the ways in which the discipline of history has become dependent on the realist paradigm; and to think through the development of historiography in consideration that all life and consciousness are one.

To decolonize history is to center historical awareness and recognize our ability to perceive and create the world that we want. Decolonizing history includes the interruption of historical practices that deny our historical awareness by imposing the realist paradigm. To decolonize history is to see that our collective understanding of history has not been of our own making. It has been made for us in such a way as to disempower our understanding of the past. Dominant historiographies do not belong to us; they have been imposed on us by the university. To delegitimize dominant practices of history is to uncover the connection between colonialism, dominant historiographies, and the university. We begin this process by naming the dominant practice of history in the university, epitomized by the life and work of Leopold von Ranke. According to Ranke, the scientific pursuit of history is the objective analysis of historical data. As the objective pursuit historical research is meant to be free of the historian's personal bias. History is understood as the excavation and study of artifacts and events. For most historians, the study of history is a straightforward practice guided by disciplinary convention and acceptable methodologies. For Ranke, historical research seeks the truth about the past. His focus on historical data suggests that for Ranke the truth lies in artifacts that existed within a particular historical context. He proposed that historical truth is to be discovered by experts relying on authentic material culture to describe particular historical events.

Ranke's scientific historiography is another example of the realist paradigm in critical theory, which is a foundational iteration of the realist paradigm in disciplined history. Unlike what Ranke believed, history is not a study of the past; nor are historical narratives about the past. History is what scholars produce according to what historians practice according to established disciplinary guidelines. For this reason, historical knowledge follows

the same patterns that Said (1979) describes for knowledge in general. Said (1979) argues
> [k]nowledge no longer requires application to reality; knowledge is what gets passed on silently, without comment, from one text to another. Ideas are propagated and disseminated anonymously, they are repeated without attribution; they have literally become *idées recues* [recited ideas]: what matters is that they are there, to be repeated, echoed, and re-echoed uncritically (116).

Historical knowledge holds no special status, it is knowledge produced in the university as all knowledge is produced in the university. History is produced according to the criteria and established parameters of the discipline. It is the historian collecting what are determined to be historical facts, and arranging them to echo the ways in which historians before him have done. The historian does not recount the truth about the past; he recites the logic of his discipline, which is the logic of the university.

The study of colonialism has succumbed to the logic of the university and is largely theorized from within the reality paradigm. In the university the study of colonialism occurs across the disciplines, producing different, and at times, contrary conceptualizations of colonialism. In the area of critical theory we have seen the emergence of scholars theorizing colonialism, postcolonialism, and settler colonialism. These concepts try to address specific situations; differentially analyzing issues of genocide, land theft, economic exploitation, imposition of a foreign aesthetic and worldview, loss of culture, language, and the attack on Indigenous social and legal structures. While scholars agree that colonialism in general includes all of these practices, they choose to create subfields in favour of dissecting what is different, particular, instead of seeking to understand what is general, universal. Within the field of colonial studies there is an emphasis on a historical analysis of 'first contact', of the initiating forces of colonialism; here we see a focus on genocide, theft of land and the politics of Empire building. In Marxist historiography the focus is to theorize these occurrences as part of the development of the capitalist mode of production. Whereas the field of postcolonialism focuses on understanding the evolution of colonial relations once countries achieve some degree of independence; they stress the ongoing a/effect of colonialism in countries no longer formally part of European Empires. In contrast, settler colonialism looks at the particular situation where the Indigenous nations have been subjugated by the settler population, where the descendant of colonizers have achieved social, political, economic, aesthetic, territorial and demographic power.

In the desire to specify the particular, the university has produced conceptualizations of coloniality that work against the possibility of conceptual convergence. If we were to focus on an analysis of the different of approaches to conceptualizing colonialism, trying to account for the particular differences that scholars stress would overwhelm us. In fact, this is the business of the university, to constantly create new fields of study, new scholarship. It does so by constantly dissecting, surgically removing parts from the whole, holding it to the light, and claiming that something new has been discovered. It is conceptual lobotomy that disregards that the whole has been shredded, that it is the scholar who has become a surgeon and has sacrificed the whole for the sake of holding up the part.

Chapter One: The realist paradigm

It is in the university where historians work and create history textbooks and writings. Therefore if we are to understand how the academic discipline of history has come into being, we need to understand the institution that structures it. We begin with the history of the university. According to most historians, the university is a uniquely European invention. This is apparently the accepted truth. However, according to the Guinness World Records the "oldest existing, and continually operating educational institution in the world is the University of Karuein founded in 859 A.D. in Fez, Morocco"[1]. Assuming that historians can also access this information, there is an important discrepancy here to unravel.

First we need to understand that most historians have a particular definition of what constitutes a university. For the most part, a university is believed to be an institution of higher learning. The experience of university is of an institution where students elect to pursue an education in a single discipline, which is understood as a distinct area of study. Dominant histories of the university narrate that the university is a European phenomenon of the modern age. In this narrative higher learning emerged at the end of the Dark Ages in European history. For Walter Rüegg "the university is a European institution; indeed it is the European institution *par excellence*" based on a community of teachers that are "accorded certain rights", have specific "objectives of research and hold publicly recognized degrees" (xix). V.H.H. Green (1974) introduces his study of Oxford University by stating, "universities were among the permanent creations of medieval civilization" (1). In their study of the history of universities Christophe Charle and Jacques (1994) claim that "as much for their institutional structure as for their social and intellectual role, universities do not have a verifiable historical precedent" (7; my translation). For most historians, the university is a uniquely European invention based on a particular lineage of philosophy and

[1] www.guinnessworldrecords.com/world-records/oldest-university

science. When historians say that the university is a European invention, what they actually mean is that based on their cultural norms and social reality higher learning originates in the model of disciplined learning.

Generally, historians of the university have a narrow vision; their sight is limited to the boundaries of Europe and more specifically, what they believe is legitimate ways of teaching and learning. For historians of the university what they define as the university in the present becomes the standard they use for their historical research. For the most part, they define the university as they have experienced it. Experiences of disciplined learning, which center on student learning based on what each discipline defines as its canon. A canon that we are told is the root of knowledge and can be traced to Ancient Greece and Rome. Every experience in the university is structured by this idea; how the disciplines are established and developed; how the institution is socially legitimated; how society supports and idealizes the university. Therefore, to understand the history of the university is to understand the history of disciplined learning.

Disciplined learning is a distinguishing feature of the European university that has been adopted beyond the space of Europe. In this model of learning, disciplines are created in relation to specialized knowledge and experts. The university is the institutionalization of these areas of knowledge and sustained by its experts. Conventional disciplines can trace their origin to medieval Europe, in particular to the "the four medical faculties of artes- variously called philosophy, letters, arts and sciences, and humanities- law, medicine, and theology have survived and have been supplemented" (Rüegg 1992, xix) where "where the general panorama of disciplines define the domain of intellectual culture" (Charle and Verger 1994, 10; my translation). Disciplines are a standard feature of the university model and collectively define what is considered to be knowledge. According to John Furlong (2013) the "term discipline [refers] to the university-based study" where "the first test of a discipline, which demands some coherence, distinctiveness and rigour in terms of epistemology" (6). This model of university learning is the separation of reality through constructed knowledge systems. Each discipline has carved out a separate area of reality, or focus of study, each having its own technical language (in the form of concepts and theories) and ways of conducting research and presenting its finding. Disciplines are manifestation of the realist paradigm in the university; it is the continued logic of dividing the world and constructing truth in the specific, particular and local interactions. In other words, each discipline has a host of legitimizing tools and techniques that justify their dissection of reality. Every surgeon-scholar dissects and sacrifices the whole to hold the part in their hands and carefully look at it to be able to speak about it as an expert.

Where you and I may be inclined to believe that every discipline is standardized- in so far as each discipline everywhere is engaging in the same (if not similar) type of scholarship- disciplines are actually quite messy. As Lloyd (2009) argues the study of the university is a "project [that] faces an immediate methodological objection. If we say that mathematics, for instance, or history, varies in different societies and at different periods, how are we to identify these non-standard varieties, and are they indeed varieties of mathematics, or history, or something else?" (2). The problem is that if we say that the defining characteristic of university learning is disciplined learning, and we cannot with any accuracy describe a discipline, then what do we do with our understanding of the university? We are then confronted by our ideological understanding of knowledge: how could this be, math is MATH, and history is HISTORY, right? Well, no. A discipline is not a natural configuration of knowledge; it is a socially constructed set of rules created by a very small group of people. As Kelley (1997) explains "[w]hat gives concreteness, continuity, and intelligibility to the history of Western Knowledge is the concept of discipline, defined originally as the relationship between disciple and master and so possessing religious as well as pedagogical and perhaps political connotation" (1). During the inception of the European university model of learning, disciplines were based on hierarchal relations, where the master instructs the disciple. It is this relationship that is the basis of European learning, of disciplined learning. What we believe a discipline to be is actually an institutionalization of a hierarchal relationship between master and disciple.

But why opt for this model of learning? It runs counter to a more idealized understanding of higher learning: the free and unrestricted pursuit of knowledge where the pedagogue is a guide on the learner's journey. It is because this model serves a particular social function. A social function is a set of "expectations [that] are based on values towards which conduct is oriented and the values are translated into norms which guide the socially expected outcome" (Rüegg 1992, xxvi). The social function of the European model of discipline learning is to create a culture of learning, which has a very specific social meaning.

> The ideas have been equally maintained that all accessible knowing resides in a certain number of texts, the respected authorities inherited from Antiquity, and that all intellectual progress could not derive except from a more profound interpretation of these texts (Charle and Verger 1994, 10; my translation).

The modern age of disciplined learning is based on the institutionalization and development of the hierarchal relation between master and disciple with the purpose of sustaining a particular set of texts as canonical. What this amounts to is the continuity of a myth. It is the myth that European knowledge, and by extension Europeaness, is rooted in the high cultures of ancient Greece and Rome. It is the sacrifice of learning for the continuation of this myth. Instead of the free pursuit of knowledge, masters discipline their students as to what to read and how to read. Degrees are awarded accordingly.

Similarly, disciplined history is not the free pursuit of knowledge about the past. It is practices that sustain historical canons and particular ideas of what history is and how to pursue historical inquiry. All of which are self-created practices of the discipline, which are sustained by the idea of historical facts. As F.H. Bradley (1968) states "the historical fact then (for us) is a conclusion; and a conclusion, however much as it may appear so, is never the fiction of a random invention" (90). What Bradley (1968) is reminding us is that there is most definitely a past to this present. We can be sure that specific events occurred, events that are the collection or constellation of facts. But what are these facts? Who decides what constitutes a historical fact? And how? For Bradley (1968) "in every case that which is called a fact is in reality a theory" (93). We have been taught that a fact is absolute. We have been taught to believe that a fact is a direct reflection of reality. Bradley suggests otherwise. Instead of a fact as direct knowledge of reality, Bradley suggests that a fact is abstract speculative knowledge of reality. Take for instance a date that we are taught is direct information of a particular day; this is for Bradley an abstract speculation. For us, every date corresponds to a date of the Gregorian calendric system. This calendar is however, an abstraction of the relationship between the sun and the earth. It is highly speculative in so far that is an inaccurate measurement of this relation- hence the need for constant corrective configurations (leap years, daylight savings). In this way, that which we believe to be a fact, such as a date on the calendar, turns out to be an abstract speculation based on a theorization which is the Gregorian calendar. We can then see that a calendar is not a definitive reflection of reality, it is better understood as a scale. A calendar is a "graduated range of values forming a standard system for measuring or grading something"[i]. Every historical date is a specific value of a calendric system- understood as a scale for the configuration of time in relation to space. As such, within a given cultural context each fact/theory, such as a calendar, is an abstraction of reality and not its reflection.

All historical narratives operate on a particular scale informed by the historian's cultural paradigm. Every historian selects his material based on that scale, and more precisely what he values on that scale. Historical narratives take shape based on the historian's assessment of the scaling of history and his determination of what has the greatest value. In other words, historical narratives are structured by the historian's configuration of reality- such as the calendric system that constitutes his understanding of space and time. This is true of all history. History is not simply facts collected and ordered by the historian. Historical narratives are based on which theories the historian subscribes to and his awareness of reality, which dictates which facts he validates ultimately resulting in his scaling of the subject matter. This process of scaling history is inherited through disciplined learning. It is embedded in the methods and methodologies that have developed according to the discipline's canons. The process of scaling history is therefore the practice of the historian. Most historians practice history without giving time to consider that this process is not only culturally specific, but the product of disciplined learning. To most it simply is the work of the historian. As such, the process is rarely discussed, and even less written about in historical narratives. To be transparent and honest about how one approaches the process of historical work, how it is that one scales history, is a crucial for the process of decolonizing history. It is to understand that decolonization is a process that begins within and extends beyond the self. Moreover, it is an acknowledgement that one's predisposition to particular facts or theories is culturally specific. History is not neutral. Decolonizing history is to recognize the political, social, economic, cultural and spiritual ramifications of one's work- which begins by including a discussion on how one scales history.

Being in the fifteenth year at the university level, there are specific ideas that have been impressed upon me. Notably, that the university is the legitimate place of knowledge, and that the core of this knowledge is European. After reading different historical accounts of the history of the university, what became clear is that the essential elements of the university's structure and processes are relatively unchanged. What struck me was the tone, or the way, that historians discuss the university. There is a sense of reverence, of epitomizing and even of loving, the institution. The overarching theme is that the university is a European institution. Regardless of how distinct the theoretical basis of different historical narratives- what the historian values in his research- the scale is of the uniquely European character of the university.

Now we know that the university as an institution of higher learning is a human phenomenon. Assuming that historians are not reckless, the discrepancy of claiming the university as uniquely European cannot be accidental - because this tendency is so pervasive among historians. It is a narrative that is consistently produced. How is it that so many historians, who may or may not know each other, perpetuate the same idea- of the university as a European invention? According to Soffer (1994), "[d]uring the past generation, the historiography of the university and its component parts has taken several distinct directions" (2); nonetheless, they all tend to arrive at the same conclusion. Each narrative of the university represents distinct processes of valuation, but all reside on the same scale. How is it then that a historian scales, or (e)valuates historical facts, events and occurrences of the past? Or, put differently, when a historian decides to write about the university, what will he choose to research, and why?

(E)valuating historical artifacts/data is the historian's process of mobilizing his own values and intentions. Generally, historians of the university write historical narratives that fall into two genres of historicizing the university as uniquely European. The first genre is a systematic approach that looks at the university model, where the research spans longer periods of time and larger geographical spaces. The valuation of this genre is based on the desire to generate statements or theories about the university model. This approach to (e)valuating historical data is driven by the belief that the truth is to be found in the abstract. The second genre researches particular universities. This approach is based on understanding the development of a specific institution over a long timeframe within a smaller expanse of space. This approach values the truth as that which is tangible.

Historians who are interested in making general statements or theories about the development of the university elect for a abstract context. Their research is not bound to a particular place or time. Two examples of this contextual approach are the historical narratives of Rüegg (1992) and Charle and Verger (1994). Rüegg (1992) is focused on defining the European university as an archetype. His research is focused on detailing what all the universities in Europe have in common. For Rüegg (1992), the

> university is a European institution because it has, in its social role, performed certain functions for all European societies. It has developed and transmitted scientific and scholarly knowledge and the methods of cultivating that knowledge which have arisen from and formed part of the common European intellectual tradition. It has at the same time formed an academic elite, which rests on common European values and which transcends all national boundaries (xx).

It is Rüegg's intention to describe the archetypal university, and what he values, which is the uniquely European quality of all universities. In contrast, Charle and Verger (1994), while sharing a similar context, are not focused on defining an archetype, but rather an ideal type.

> The first universities, as indicated in our introduction, appeared in occidental Europe at the beginning of the XIII century. Notwithstanding that we cannot assign a specific date of their inception, we can consider the contemporaneous universities of Bologna, Paris, and Oxford to be similar (Charle and Verger 1994, 7; my translation).

Charle and Verger's research is focused on the universities of Oxford, Paris, and Bologna as examples of the ideal typology of the European university. Their focus is, within a general temporal and spatial context, to underscore both the similarities and differences among their specific examples to be able to define an ideal typology. In their historical analysis they conclude that

> These first universities did not follow a unique model. From the beginning, we are presented with two very distinct pedagogical and institutional systems. In the northern half of Europe (Paris, Oxford), universities were primarily associations of teachers, or, if one prefers, a federation of schools; the dominant disciplines were the liberal arts and theology while the ecclesial imprint remained strong. Most students were, with exception of the school of arts, very young. In the Mediterranean countries, universities were above all associations of students, where teachers were more or less excluded. The teachable disciplines were the law, medicine, which implied that the average age of students was older and that they were of a higher social status. And if a certain ecclesial control succeeded to impose itself, it disappointedly remained beyond the institution itself (Charle and Verger 1994, 12-13; my translation).

For Charle and Verger the ideal typology of the university is based on certain traits they hold in common. These common traits include the universities foundations as associations, disciplinary structure and relationship to the Christian faith. Despite the same historical scaling of the university, and the similar general context, these historians offer different historical narratives of the development of the university model. Rüegg (1992) stresses the similarity of all European universities, while Charle and Verger (1994) point to three instances of an ideal typology, noting that they share both similarities and differences in their development.

Another genre of writing the history of the university is to focus on specific institutions, over a long temporal frame. In his book *La Sorbonne* Alfred Franklin (1968) in documenting the inception of the Sorbonne in Paris, focuses on its principle founder, Robert Sorbonensis, a Chaplin of Saint Louis. Franklin's (1968) account is based on research of how Robert Sorbonensis acquired buildings that were to become the university grounds. In contrast we have Green's (1974) book *A history of Oxford University*. Green's (1974) research is a compilation of historical data about Oxford's facilities, scholarly development, architecture, administrative and accreditation processes, its litigation with nearby towns and its relationship to the king and Church. While Green (1974) establishes that the universities at Paris and Bologna as contemporaries of Oxford university, his focus is on what he believes in unique about Oxford. Despite the same historical scaling of the university, and the similar context, these historians offer different historical narratives of the development of La Sorbonne and Oxford universities. Franklin (1968) is interested in underscoring the condition of possibility for the emergence of La Sorbonne in Paris, namely the work and commitment of Robert Sorbonensis. In contrast, Green's (1974) more detailed account of all aspects of the development of Oxford University gives an in-depth analysis, from inception to the present moment.

What then is the truth about the history of the university? It is best narrated as an archetype, ideal type, or is the truth to be found in the particulars of each institution? Furthermore, if all of these narratives belong to the discipline of history- in so far as they have been researched and written by historians trained in the methods and best practices of the discipline- why so many distinct narratives? Furthermore, given all of the different approaches and narratives of the history of the university, how is it that all these historians share the same idea of the university as a uniquely European phenomenon?

Rüegg's history of the university is extreme in this belief. For him the university is quintessentially European in its quality and development, his narrative never betrays or diverges from this proposition. Charle and Verger, while maintaining the Europeaness of the university, have moments that quietly suggest something else to the reader, without elaborating the point. In their study, they state that

> The XIII century we saw a new wave of translations of Aristotle, accompanied by their Arab commentaries of the highest prestige (Avienne, Avverroes). With these texts [came] more than simply logic, like in the XII century; it was from this moment that the unity of Greco-Arabic philosophy and science

> became accessible and suddenly appeared in the Occidental school (Charle and Verger 1994, 14; my translation).

Green (1974) implicitly echoes this point when he writes that "a revolution was taking place in twelfth-century Europe, generating everywhere a zest for intellectual enquiry which the existing cathedral and monastic schools could not meet" (1). Elsewhere Green (1974) notes that

> By the close of the fourteenth century Oxford's prestige in the world scholarship stood high. The university had come into being at a time when the character of medieval learning was itself being shaped anew. The narrower theological concepts, so strongly influenced by the ideas of the fifth-century African, St Augustine of Hippo, were giving way to a broader synthesis in which the re-discovered philosophy of Aristotle has a major part to play (15).

In these obscure moments of these texts, there is evidence presented that the development of the university had both African and Arabic influence. African and Arabic influence within the university is casually mentioned and under theorized. There is within this literature a simultaneous subtle acknowledgement and overwhelming disavowal of the Other's influence in the development of the university. There are moments in the texts that mention this influence, but these moments are not part of the larger historical narrative. They dismiss the Other by explaining these moments as European in character. Such is the case when Kelley (1997) writes

> Historical scholarship had long supplemented philosophical speculation in the effort to understand human nature in its widest sense; the exploration of the New World provided no less exotic examples of human diversity; and it was out of this growing mass of ethnographic data and its increasing sophisticated analysis that this new discipline developed and that the human science more generally expanded (7).

The lives, philosophy and culture of the Other never appear in the text; thereby denying African, Arabic and Indigenous agency and creativity. It is also a denial of the significance of African, Arabic and Indigenous knowledge and ways of knowing to the development of the European university. When reading these texts one may be more inclined to believe that the influence of the Other was more the result of European ingenuity and innovation rather than part of a larger politicized project that has been nearly erased from dominant historical narratives.

The significance or occurrence of the Other's influence in the development of the European university cannot be denied. Even among scholars that premise their scholarship on the uniquely European character of the university, this influence is still embedded in most of these narratives- albeit insignificantly. Instead of narrating *the* history of the university, what these historians of the university have done is write about the ideology of a unique Europe. There have been many, like Said, who have argued that Europe is an idea. This idea is an ideology that holds sway over many people. Just as with all ideology, it is not just an idea. It is an idea that serves a social function. David Harvey (2001) explains this social function as a 'geographic lore'. For Harvey (2001)

> [a]ll societies, classes, and social groups possess a distinctive 'geographic lore', a working knowledge of their territory, of the spatial configuration of use values relevant to them, and of how they may intervene to shape the use values to their own purposes. This 'lore', acquired through experience, is codified and socially transmitted as part of a conceptual apparatus with which individuals and groups cope with the world. It may take the form of a loosely-defined spatial and environmental imagery or of a formal body of knowledge - geography - in which all members of society or a privileged elite receive instruction. This knowledge can be used in the struggle to liberate peoples from 'natural' disasters and constraints and from external oppression. It can be used in the quest to dominate nature and other peoples and to construct an alternative geography of social life through the shaping of physical and social environments for social ends (108-9).

For Harvey, geographic knowledge amounts to a specific awareness of oneself, one's culture in relation to a constructed geographic space. This awareness is social, it forms a cultural apparatus; a communal awareness that becomes how a society knows itself, where it is, and who does not belong. Furthermore, geographic lore is a particular imaginary, a way to legitimize a politicized occupation of space. The belief of the university as a uniquely European institution is part of a European conceptual apparatus; it is the belief that there is knowledge that is European, and that the study and development of knowledge has been conducted in a European way. All of which is sustained by one central imaginary: of a discreet and distinct geographical space of Europe that has produced the university in an insular way.

In the university the colonial iteration conceals the context of Empire, and colonialism as a fundamental part of its development; a concealment dependent on the 'lore of Europe'. The 'lore' of Europe is an imaginary that manifests as an experienced geography, which functions as a paradigm. The fact of geography, an imagined unified space, creates a conceptual framework, a frame of mind that defines and explains reality based on the idea of Europe. It is an idea that becomes prescriptive and descriptive of reality. Harvey's (2001) concept of a geographic lore allows us to understand how scholars who write very different histories of the development of the university hold the same belief that the institution is uniquely European. We are not talking about a conspiracy theory, but rather a particular cultural awareness that creates an imaginary that anything within the space of Europe must be European. The notion of cultural exchange or cultural appropriation is not readily considered. In fact it is shunned. But what if the matter of cultural exchange or cultural appropriation were the focus of a history of the development of the university?

If one's awareness is of a distinct and discreet Europe, than one's historical awareness will be of a distinct and discreet European history. We see this in the literature of the history of the university. The history of Europe as a distinct area of historical scholarship separate from colonialism is testament to this belief. The history of Europe's Others is never the history of Europe in dominant narratives. There exists a definite separation in dominant research between what happened in Europe- and can therefore be identified as European history- and what Europeans did elsewhere- which becomes the history of those Other places. These Other places are denied their own histories, their own experiences. If Europeans have been involved, these Other places become defined by that encounter. However, these encounters are not taken into account in European history. European history is stand-alone. There is a failure to understand the reality of cultural exchange, of how both spaces and peoples interact. In the pursuit to identify and write the history of the uniquely European university there is a simultaneous disavowal of how this institution has been marked and created through encounters with African, Arabic and Indigenous nations.

How is it that we have such a specific understanding of Europe, not only as an insular space, but also as unaffected by all of their international activities, by their colonization of Other nations? To some extent we all share this idea; I know I did with respect to the development of the university. I have believed Europe to be a space with a long history of philosophy, traditions, of innovation, of a unique intellectual culture, expressed in art, knowledge, and social organization. I have never been to Europe, so I have never been able to attest or bear witness to anything that I have believed. But I believed it nonetheless. I am concerned with understanding how this geographical lore has come to be believed by so many of us. In the case of the university, how most scholars have- myself included- come to hold the belief that it is a uniquely European institution. We are faced with a situation where higher learning has become synonymous with the European university. Universities, wherever they are, are imagined to have their roots in a distinctively European genealogy of knowledge production. As we have seen, the idea of a uniquely European university has not spontaneously appeared, historians have produced it. Harvey (2001) argues, "the form and content of geographic knowledge cannot be understood independently of the social basis for the production and use of that knowledge" (109). The idea of Europe, as a distinct and discreet space, with unique institutions, is being intentionally produced. In this situation, those of us who have immersed their lives in the university have a responsibility to understand what we are participating in. We have a responsibility to know the social basis of use of the myth of the uniquely European university.

This geographic lore, as it sustains the idea of the uniquely European university, conceals how appropriated knowledge, converted into intellectual property, has developed the university from its inception while supporting imperial projects. Yet, dominant histories of the university do not include a discussion or analysis of colonialism in the development of the university; in particular how the Other's knowledge was appropriated by way of colonialism, conquest and plunder. History is written in a way that obscures this relationship. Historiography- the way history is scaled and historical facts (e)valuated- is based on processes to disavow colonialism. In contrast, a decolonizing critical historiography includes a focus on the analysis of these iterative processes. It is an approach to history that is primarily concerned with understanding colonialism. This book asks: what would it mean to have a historiography of the coloniality of the university?

In discussing the practice of history, that is, occurrences in the past, we cannot be sure what actually happened. Nonetheless, it is possible to account for the past. In this way, we do not search for the truth, but rather, we focus on the criteria for historical analysis. In this search we evaluate the beliefs of the historian as to what constitutes history. Instead of verifying facts, we scrutinize the presuppositions of the historian. For instance, we ask why Europe is the geography for the history of the university. How is it that conquest and plunder escape notice or acknowledgement? By what criteria are facts believed? How do historians decide how far back to look when they begin their research? We also scrutinize the way historians construct history because we know that like us, they are human beings. As human beings, they are guided by their beliefs and intentions. Therefore, we also want to understand their motivations, and how these motivations dictate the choices they make in how and what they research and write. At a basic level, we recognize that to focus intentionally on one aspect of the story is simultaneously an erasure of the other side of the story. While historians fixated on narrating the university as a uniquely European institution they were simultaneously erasing how conquest and plunder of Other spaces were essential and necessary for the development of the university. In other words, we focus on how the dominant history of the university unilaterally disavows the context of colonialism.

To do this asks of us to consider how and why knowledge is produced. It requires that we understand what is considered knowledge, how it becomes institutionalized, and what its role is in society. To understand the production of the idea of the university as uniquely European is

> [t]he study of the active construction and transformation of material environments (both physical and social) together with critical reflection on the production and use of geographic knowledge within the context of that activity, could become the center of concern. The focus is on the process of becoming through which people (and geographers) transform themselves through transforming both their natural and social milieu (Harvey 2001, 115).

For Harvey, understanding what we know about nature and society is to understand how we are becoming ourselves. In this way the search of understanding our relation to the university, which has been engulfed in the lore of Europe, is a deeply personal one. It involves our motivation as we shape how we know who we are and where we are.

The motivation of historians that narrate dominant narratives of the university is shaped by their belief in the idea of Europe; it is how the lore of Europe has cast its spell. As people living in Europe, the motivation of knowledge production is predominantly focused on becoming European, on exploring themselves and their history based on the idea of Europe. Now, as we have seen, dominant historical narratives do not adequately account or discuss the presence of the Other as part of the knowledge production process in European universities. However, when this occurrence of the

Other is acknowledged it is mentioned briefly in passing and never taken into account in the overall narrative or analysis. We can however access this dismissed history in alternative narratives of the university. These alternative narratives include a discussion of the European appropriation of the Other's knowledge and systems for knowledge production.

Although dominant historical narratives do not dispute the Other's presence in the development of the university alternative narratives about colonialism are generally dismissed. This institutional marginalization is a consequence of the lore of Europe, the belief in a Europe free of non-Europeans. When we center these alternative narratives we see that this belief is not only being produced, it is covering-up an essential part of the history of the university. The lore of Europe dictates that knowledge production is essentially, culturally, stylistically, and intellectually only ever European. To consider the university as a uniquely European institution one needs to establish particular criteria for historical analysis. One must establish Europe as the site of such an analysis. Research is then conducted based on the historian's experience, what the historian understands a university to be based on his own education. This is likely tied to the hierarchal teaching and learning of established canons. Once the discipline of history has established its methods and canon within the realist paradigm, only then can the historical narratives erase the guild of masters and disciples as their preference for Arabic knowledge runs counter to the belief as to what forms the basis of European canons- namely Greek philosophy and its subsequent development. Historians can also ignore the social function of the university in Empire, the role of botanists, as the idea of Europe dictates that colonialism has no place in the history of Europe, let alone in the history of the university. This is the process of most historians of the university. However, if one chooses to focus on the guild of masters in their challenge to the feudal order and the church, of the long standing tradition of the university's appropriation of African, Arabic and Indigenous knowledge, one may be inclined to think of the university as intimately connected to conquest and plunder, of being in collusion with Empire and being a primary resource and project of the Imperial apparatus.

PART THREE:
History disciplined

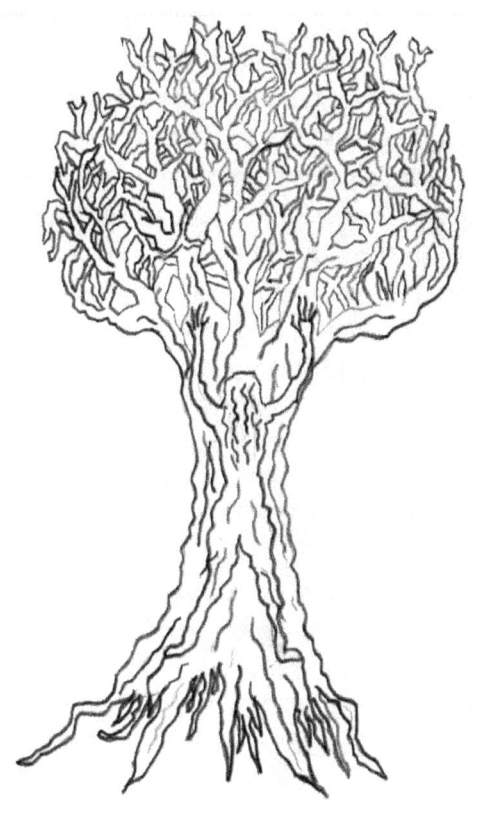

Decolonizing history is to confront the logic of realism. To understand how and why it holds power over us, to see the ways in which this logic has not only disciplined how we understand the past, but also our relationship to what has been. According to the OED, logic is "reasoning conducted or assessed according to strict principles of validity"[ii]. Logic is therefore, not a straightforward process of assessment or reasoning. Logic is reason inhibited and constrained by what has been established to be valid. Or put another way, logic is the practice of making reasonable what has been institutionally validated. In the context of the university, logic makes reasonable the validation of the realist paradigm. One foundational iteration of the realist paradigm is the delegitimization of Indigenous modalities. It is the logic of making reasonable the belief that Indigenous social structures, cosmologies, and ways of knowing are invalid. Another iteration of the realist paradigm functions as the logic of creating a world divided. It is the logic of hierarchy, of duality. It is the logic of the inferior Native and superior European. The university is premised on the belief of the superiority of Euro-American philosophy and knowledge. In reality, the university is a primary site of coloniality. As Byrd (2011) argues, within

> the matrix of critical theory, Indianness moves not through absence but through reiterations, through meme, as theories circulate and fracture, quote and build. The prior ontological concerns that interpellate Indianness and savagery as ethnographic evidence and example, lamentable and tragic loss, are deferred through repetitions (xviii).

Critical theory is based on the repetition of Indian savagery. The reiterations of *Indianess* become the ontological foundation for establishing critical theory. For Byrd (2011) there would not be critical theory without the anchor of *Indianess*. The presupposition of critical theory in the university is the continuous invalidation of Indigeneity. Indigenous absence and ideological inscription becomes the condition of possibility for the emergence of critical theory.

Decolonizing history, the confrontation of its logic, begins by naming these simultaneous processes of invalidating *Indianess* and validating critical theory as a uniquely and exclusively Euro-American creation. To decolonize history is to explore the ways in which the university has proliferated this idea. In particular, how the university has propagated itself through appropriating and manipulating Indianess. Decolonizing history also necessitates that we establish a new relationship to Indigeneity and refuse the continuous invalidation of Indigenous modalities. Decolonizing history begins with perceiving our relationality to Indigenous nations as we account for our obligation to Indigenous law and legal structures, and that we tell that story- of coming to ourselves as Treaty people.

Decolonizing history is to learn about treaties. This necessitates that one unlearn history as we know it. It is to critically examine the dominant narrative of the founding of nations, to understand that the coming into being of nation-states occurs through genocide and theft of land. In the context of the Canada, the rise of the nation-state has meant the creation of borders that seek to dismantle Indigenous international relations between sovereign nations. It is the deliberate attempt to halt Indigenous economies, trade routes and complex ideas of extended kinship ties. Moreover, borders seek to erase from awareness the cosmologies of the land, the sacred knowledges of Turtle Island, of Abya Yala and of their relation. To unlearn Canadian history is to understand that what we have been taught to be history is in fact colonial propaganda. Decolonizing history is to learn about the colonization of Turtle Island and the role of the Canadian state, its policies and practices that continue to create new methods and avenues for genocide. To know the history of Canadian colonization is to understand that the state and its citizens are in violation of Treaties.

Therefore, for someone to understand their obligation to these agreements requires that one know the nation they belong to. In this way, decolonizing history is to decolonize how we know ourselves, our relation to the Canadian state, and our responsibility to Indigenous law and legal structures. Decolonizing history begins as we understand our personal and collective experiences of colonialism and the reasons and ways in which we have internalized dominant narratives of colonization. This process requires that we understand the role of the university in disseminating dominant historical narratives of colonization as well as know about the social function of the university with respect to colonialism.

A decolonizing history rejects realism, in particular the analytic priority of matter. To decolonize historiography puts into question the normative ideas of time and space, which have been ideologically created to invalidate Indigenous, African and traditional cosmologies of dynamic time and motion. A decolonizing history recognizes the unity of matter and consciousness, and seeks to narrate this unity.

Chapter Two: From materialism to iteration

The materialist conception of history is an alternative historiography. This is because Marx and Engels' approach to history focuses on the exploitation of workers and the internal contradictions of the capitalist mode of production with the purpose of narrating the ultimate outcome of historical development of capitalism to be the inception of socialism. In this respect, the materialist conception of history provides a developmental approach to history; it narrates the past leading to a prophetic outcome as a necessary remedy to the irrational mode of production and exchange of capitalism. In "Theoretical, Engels (1939) argues that the

> materialist conception of history starts from the proposition that the production and, next to production, the exchange of things produced, is the basis of all structures; that in every society that has appeared in history, the manner in which wealth is distributed and society divided into classes or estates is dependent upon what is produced, how it is produced, and how the products are exchanged (1).

Marx and Engels offer an approach to history that is universal. Engels (1939) argues that every society is structured by the economic infrastructure by which products are made and distributed. To further explain this approach, Engels (1939) narrated the transition from feudalism to capitalism. He explains how under the economic structure of feudalism, people produced what they needed for themselves and their families, where any surplus was traded; a situation of individual production and individual appropriation. As people were violently taken off the land, and the introduction of new technology, individual producers were forced into the labour market and became wage-labourers. Workers laboured for a wage, which they used to purchase the products they and their families needed. The owners of the means of production, those who owned the factories, machines and materials needed to make commodities, owned the product of the worker's labour, which they sold for a profit; a situation of social production and individual (or capitalist) appropriation.

Engels (1939) explains how the situation of social production and individual (or capitalist) appropriation is the first contradiction of capitalism, the exploitation of the workers labour and profiteering of capitalist, causing a situation of class conflict: workers against bourgeois capitalists. Engels (1939) explains how from this contradiction arise two subsequent contradictions internal to the capitalist mode of production. The second contradiction is "between the organization of production in the individual factory and the anarchy of production in society as a whole" (Engels 1939, 299). Engels (1939) is describing the situation where individual capitalists organize production in their factories with utmost efficiency, meaning that the factory is set up to produce the optimal amount of commodities in the shortest amount of time in the most cost-effective way. However, within capitalism there is no one, or no group of people, regulating or monitoring what is being produced at the level of society. Therefore production occurs in a way that is unstructured, with no concern that social needs are being met. This is a situation of anarchy of production because while there is organized production in the individual factory, there is a lack of organization at the level of society. This leads to what Engels (1939) describes as the third contradiction of the capitalist mode of production; where "the mode of production rebels against the mode of exchange; the productive forces rebel against the mode of production, which they have outgrown" (302). Engels (1939) explains how it is that capitalists, in their eternal quest to increase their profits, seek to reduce costs by constantly seeking time and cost saving technologies. These productive forces, new machinery for example, take over production leading to a decreased need for wage-labourers. In this prophetic scenario, when in a society technology has permanently displaced workers, the products being produced will not enter the circuits of exchange as workers will no longer be able to buy commodities. The third contradiction leads to a situation where Marx and Engels believed that workers would rebel. In this rebellion workers would take control of the means of production and the state, expropriate capitalists, and socialize the production and exchange of commodities. This ideal outcome of the capitalist mode of production, socialism, would ensure that all people would receive what they needed and usher in a new freedom from tedious work and introduce the possibility of leisure and pleasure. In this way, the materialist conception of history is based on the analysis of the factory in relation to society. The social, for Marx and Engels is conceptualized realistically; it is the local space of minute interactions. The social is cut off from the totality of relations that inform and constitute society as it is.

The materialist conception of history is appealing because it seems reasonable in so far as it is premised on that which is tangible and quantifiable, the circulation of commodities in society. It is appealing because this approach explores the root of economic exploitation realistically. Marx and Engels' historical narratives develop based on the principles of strong objectivity and causality. Their narratives give meaning to tangible and quantifiable social relations. The parameters of their narratives formulate historical events as necessary precursors that account for the totality of economic relations of their present time. In this way, for Marx and Engels, capitalism is a necessary condition for the emergence of socialism. For Engels (1939) it was the historic role of capitalist production to seize control of the economy and force the reality of social production.

> (In the middle ages the) instruments of labour- land, agricultural implements, the workshop, the tool- were the instruments of labour of single individuals, adapted for these of one workers, and therefore, of necessity, small, dwarfish, circumscribed. But, for this very reason they belonged, as a rule, to the producer himself. To concentrate these scattered, limited means of production, to enlarge them, to turn them into the powerful levers of production of the present day- this was precisely the historic role of capitalist production and of its upholder, the bourgeoisie. In Part IV of Capital, Marx has explained in detail, how since the fifteenth century this has been historically worked out through the three phases of simple

co-operation, manufacture and modern industry (Engels 1939, 2).

Theoretical, its historical account of the transition from feudalism and to capitalism is grounded by Marx's analysis of the emergence of social production. For Marx and Engels, capitalism is not the problem, but rather, the condition of possibility for the emergence of socialism. Socialism is dependent on the development of efficient social production, which the capitalist mode of production has made possible. This is a historical account which both explains and justifies the materialist conception of history.

The materialist conception of history accounts for economic relations within a local context in a strict causality that develops a progressive narrative of human history. Marx and Engels, in their narrow vision of the progress of humanity and idealization of socialism, ignore Marx's marginalization of the historical context for the production of surplus-value (Skillman 2013), the role of consumption (Harvey 2012) and the state (Banaji 2013) in capitalism. Moreover, in their focus on a fundamental materialism, Marx and Engels do not, or cannot, account for or address the role of nature in the ontological and cosmological constitution of the economy.

The materialist conception of history is premised on the idea that an economy is contingent on the production and exchange of commodities, and that to understand a society is to understand the economy in this way. However, what this premise ignores is that an economy cannot exist without a pre-existing relation to nature. In other words, the way that a society understands and relates to nature forms the basis on its economic order as well as the possibility of what economies can develop, which is dependent on the ontological status of nature in society as well the cosmological underpinning of that ontology. This is not to say that Marx does not consider nature in his critique of political economy, because he does. Marx employs the concept of metabolism to discuss nature, which draws on the work of chemist Jutus Von Liebig. Liebig's research was on soil chemistry, he employed the term metabolism to explore the nutrient cycle of soil (Foster 2000, 149-54). He observed how certain agricultural practices depleted the soil of specific nutrients, which required replenishing through fertilization. Marx appropriated this concept to discuss how human beings are connected to nature. For Marx the primary feature of human beings is their sociability, understood as a metabolic relation of human beings to the land; "This originates from the fact that man, if not as Aristotle thought a political animal, is at all events a social animal" (Marx 1976, 444). Therefore, nature enters the frame of his analysis at the social level. As Marx (1976) writes

> [i]t is an appropriation of what exists in nature for the requirements of man. It is the universal condition for the metabolic interaction (Stoffwechsel) between man and nature, the everlasting nature-imposed condition of human existence, and is therefore independent of every form of that existence; or rather it is common to all forms of society in which human beings live (290).

For Marx, there is no disconnect between human beings and nature, human beings exists because they intimately interact and appropriate aspects of nature into our own being; a quality that is for Marx universal.

This is however, the extent to which Marx involves nature in his analysis of political economy. For the most part, the concept of metabolism is a "biological analogy (that) plays a considerable part of his analysis of circulation and the labour process" (Marx 1976, 198). Marx borrows from Liebig's research the idea of metabolism as an analogy for the circulation of commodities in society. As he explains,

> In so far as the process of exchange transfers commodities from hands in which they are non-use-values to hands in which they are use-values, it is a process of social metabolism. The product of one kind of useful labour replaces that of another. Once a commodity has arrived at a situation in which it can serve as a use-value, it falls out of the sphere of exchange into that of consumption (Marx 1976, 290).

When Marx employs the concept of metabolism to society, it is no longer a biological condition of existence but a literary analogy. In this way, for Marx social metabolism is a figurative term in so far as he does not theorize the biological or ontological conditions that sustain a society's economy. As a result, he does not consider the role of nature, or how and what human beings appropriate from nature, or why. Marx did not, or could not, apprehend that the capitalist mode of production could never arise from within societies that have a highly developed agricultural sciences based on a sacred relation to the land. While Marx and Engels first believed that traditional cultures were primitive and therefore had not yet developed the capitalist impulse, what they could not be aware of, because of the state of their culture's scientific awareness, was the African, Indigenous and traditional peoples would never develop a capitalist economy as it is contrary to their cosmologies. Furthermore, the capitalist mode of production contradicts their scientific, philosophical and ontological awareness, that were sustainable and more reliable.

Moreover, this tendency to downplay or ignore the role of nature is prominent in the production process as outlined in Part IV of Capital. This is evidenced by Marx's focus on mechanization as that which is centrally important in the development of the production process because, as he argues, increased technology increases the productivity of workers while decreasing wages, all of which amount to overall increase in productivity and surplus value; thereby ignoring how capitalism appropriates from nature in a violent and unsustainable way through relations of coloniality. According to Marx, the process of production under the capitalist mode of production is simultaneously the production of surplus value. For Marx, the capitalist mode of production is based on a fundamental contradiction of the exploitation of workers by capitalist who appropriate profit as the commodities that workers produce enter the circuits of exchange.

To accompany the materialist conception of history that focuses on the production and exchange of commodities, in *Capital* Marx sought to articulate a comprehensive theory of surplus value specific to the capitalist mode of production. The development of his theoretical analysis is not, however straightforward. As Gilbert L. Skillman (2013) points out, Marx's theory of surplus-value as it appears in *Capital* was subject to radical revision from previous drafts of *Capital*. In his research Skillman (2013) sought to discuss

> Marx's analysis of the systemic conditions' underlying capitalists appropriation of *surplus value*, his term for the general economic category yielding profit, interest, and rent as specific expressions. Marx's analysis on this point features two distinct lines of argument that in previous work I have labelled his *value-theoretic*[2] and *historical*[3] accounts of surplus value (476).

In his analysis of Marx's drafts and final version of *Capital*, Skillman (2013) concluded that Marx deployed two distinct approaches to understanding the production of surplus value. Marx's value-theoretic approach was focused on elaborating a theory that was universally true of the capitalist mode of production while his historical approach analyzed specific situations to understand the production of surplus-value. Presumably, he intended the two accounts to be mutually consistent if not complementary; they are in any case intertwined and accorded more or less equal

> expository status in the first two drafts of Capital... (Nonetheless) Marx decided to alter dramatically the relative status of the two accounts, introducing a number of revisions that served to downplay and obscure his historical account of

---

[2] Value-theoretic account: "seeks to explain the economic basis of surplus value in terms of a theorized relationship between commodity prices and their respective values" (Skillman 2013, 477).

[3] Historical account: "investigates developments in the capacity of capitalists to extract surplus value on the basis of temporally given conditions of production and exchange, without positing any particular relationship between commodity prices and values. (This account) is comprised of two analytically related narratives, one concerning the ability of capitalists to appropriate surplus value in the absence of any direct control of the production process ... and the other regarding the ability of capitalists to extract surplus value when they do control the labor process" (Skillman 2013, 477).

surplus value relative to its value-theoretic counterpart (Skillman 2013, 477).

In his revision of *Capital* Marx omitted or downplayed historical evidence in favour of the development of a comprehensive theory.

Harvey (2012) explains this focus on the development of theory to be a strategic commitment for Marx. Harvey (2012) writes: "[m]y best hypothesis is that if Marx's fundamental aim was to critique classical political economy in its own terms then he had to accept the general nature of those terms in order to identify their inner contradictions and deconstruct their absences" (11). This was Marx's primary objective in writing, to mount a substantial theoretical critique of the dominant political economy of his time. Moreover, "Marx argued, it is necessary to rely on abstraction to arrive at foundational concepts" (Harvey 2012, 6). For Marx, the best strategy to dispel the problematic and what he saw as dangerous currents in economic paradigms of his time was to construct a comprehensive political economy based on a conceptual analysis of the capitalist mode of production; henceforth his focus on developing foundational concepts and theory. Aside from the historical analysis that does not make a significant appearance in the final version of *Capital*, there is also a general tendency to treat historical occurrences with less scholarly rigor than the theoretical suppositions of the text. In other words, the historical narratives in *Capital* are superficial in comparison to the in-depth development of theoretical concepts. As Harvey (2012) argues, there is "a seemingly unbridgeable divide between the fluid, accidental and voluntaristic tone of the historical writings on the one had and the works of rigorously scientific and law-like political economy on the other" (4). Leading Harvey (2012) to conclude that "we may infer that Marx views 'history' on the one hand and economics and the critique of political economy on the other as two distinguishable, if not separate, fields of inquiry" (4) where these "hints point towards a desire to construct the purest possible theory of a capitalist mode of production, uncontaminated by any attempt at grounding it anywhere" (8). According to Harvey, Marx saw clarity in theory, and messiness in history. Marx preferred theory, as it best suited his intention to mount a destabilizing critique of a problematic political economy. In the historical occurrences, Marx found difference and situations that did not neatly fit the concepts he was developing; the outcome being a pragmatic decision to omit critical historical analysis from *Capital*.

There are two direct and significant consequences of Marx's decision to disengage a rigorous historical analysis. A lack of analysis of the historical occurrences leads to an absence of a "theory of an evolving consumerism is Capital" (Harvey 2012, 3). For Harvey this glaring omission is problematic since the "manipulation and mobilization of human desires has been central to the history of capitalism, but Marx excludes it from the political economy precisely because it is the work of history to deal with!" (Harvey 2012, 20). This omission diverts attention away from an analysis of human consciousness and cosmologies in structuring how people live, desire and consume. Secondly, a lack of historical clarity obscures the role of the state in the development and continuity of the capitalist mode of production. To this exclusion Banaji (2013) "argues that Marxists should see history as being driven by the state as much as it is by classes"(129). A failure to concretely focus on the state is a failure to understand how Empire functions to regulate and support the capitalist mode of production.

To include a historically grounded analysis of consumption and the state may complete Marx's analysis. In particular, it may shed light on the two key implications that Skillman (2013) identifies that have been obscured in Marx's turn to theory and dismissal of history. Skillman (2013) argues that the

> alterations in Marx's historical account had the effect of obscuring two key implications that are repeatedly expressed in the prepublication drafts of Capital: first, capitalists were historically able to secure surplus value without hiring wage labor and exercising direct control over the production process, even during the era of industrial capitalism; second, and

> consequently, the connection between capitalist control of production processes employing wage labor and realization of surplus value is not categorical and a matter of necessity, as suggested in K.1, but contingent and a matter of degree (478).

Furthermore, "Marx's historical account identifies scenarios in which specific disparities of commodity prices and values are necessary for the realization of surplus value, but capitalist control of production and the purchase of wage labor are not" (Skillman 2013, 480). Skillman (2013) explains how Marx's historical accounts are contradictory to his conceptualization of the production of surplus value. Under the capitalist mode of production, argues Marx, capitalist control the production process (ownership of the means of production, and hiring of wage-labourers) a scenario which is necessary condition for the production of surplus value. Therefore the historical accounts Marx omitted not only disrupt how production is conceptualized, but also how surplus-value is theorized as well as how he sought to explain the relationship between the production process and the production of surplus value.

The materialist conception of history stipulates that a study of history that seeks to understand the social structures and their development ought to focus its attention on the production and exchange of commodities. However, as Harvey (2012) points out, Marx neglects any real analysis of the exchange of commodities in favour of focusing of the production process. As Harvey (2012) argues the "textual evidence is irrefutable that Marx's political economy operates primarily and frequently exclusively at the level of the law-like generality of production. Why the priority of production?" (14). On a practical level it is easy to understand this priority. Given Marx's intention to offer a critic, the best way he must have seen is to provide a concrete theoretical analysis; hence, the focus on production. The production process, including the means of production, the reality of wage-workers in factories for instance, are easily studied, qualitatively and quantitatively analyzed, offering rich material for the development of concepts. In other words, the focus on the production process was a practical decision, as it is more manageable to analyze a factory, than for example, it is to trace the life-cycle of a commodity from its natural beginnings to its appearance in the circuits of exchange, which may span vast spaces, over a complex temporal context. It is for this reason that we see in *Capital* a localized analysis of the production process, dismissing elements of the production process over complex geographical and temporal contexts. For as Marx (1976) himself admits, "the spreading-out of work over great areas and the great number of people employed in each branch of labour obscures the connection" (475). It would seem that Marx saw the task of a comprehensive analysis of the production process as an insurmountable task in the way that he wanted to do it; which led to a detailed study of specific processes in a particular space over a relative short and simple temporal context. A situation that led Marx to develop concepts and a theoretical paradigm in lieu of an analysis of the production process in a way that is inclusive of all workers and all levels of production and exchange.

As we have seen, "Marx's value-theoretic and historical accounts of surplus value were mutually inconsistent on critical theoretical points" (Skillman 2013, 480). By focusing on the development of capitalism in a particular area of Western Europe, and Britain in particular, Marx effectively erases the full context of the capitalist mode of production. In his discussion of the production process Marx's focus is on localized developments, capitalist use of new technologies and treatment of workers in the factory. What is crucially missing in this scenario is the raw materials that technologies and workers made use of to produce commodities. This has very specific implications for Marx's theoretical development. Firstly, it ignores the conditions and situations by which raw materials are made available for the production process. Secondly, it ignores the international network of capitalists and the role of imperial states in facilitating the use of raw materials for the production process. Lastly, it ignores how raw materials are a significant part of the production process to the extent of being a determining aspect of the production of surplus value. Harvey (2012) puts this as follows: "Consumption cannot, therefore, be kept entirely outside of political economy as a general category because it reacts 'upon the point of departure of capital accumulation and initiates the whole process anew'" (19). What Harvey (2012) fails to acknowledge is that while it is true that consumption is a necessary component of the cycle of production, it is also an fundamental feature of colonialism.

It would be problematic to reject or dismiss Marx and Engels, or to ignore the significance of the materialist conception of history. However, it would be equally problematic to ignore how it is that Marx disavows the colonial context of the development of the capitalist mode of production. In ignoring consumption, specifically the conditions of how and what raw materials furnished European industry on a large scale, what is being disavowed is colonialism. It is the processes of colonialism, of biocolonialism, of extraction of plant materials from the colonies, the state administered international development of botany and technologies for the optimal commodification of plant materials, that made possible the development of capitalism as it occurred in the space of Western Europe. Moreover, by disregarding colonialism what is being ignored is the central role of the institution of slavery in colonialism, and the development of capitalism. As Banaji (2013) suggests "that the real reason why Marx had to acknowledge the capitalist nature of plantations was the impact of the colonial trades on the equalization of the general rate of profit, in particular their role in 'raising the general level of profit" (138). Not only did the plantation economy furnish European industry with raw materials necessary for the production process, it was in and of itself capitalist. Banaji (2013) further argues, "modern slavery can be seen as a purely capitalist institution, since 'the business in which slaves (were) used (was) conducted by capitalists'" (129). Henceforth what developed on a world-wide scale was an international network of capitalists; profiteering from the plantation economy and the European economy, forming one global economic network; all of which was supported and mediated by Empire.

It is fair to say that Marx sacrificed a complete understanding of the development of the capitalist mode of production in favour of delegitimizing the dominant political theories of his day. In doing so he also sacrificed the stories, the lived realities, of colonialism. He settled for the prospect of the eventual liberation of the proletariat, instead of truly revolutionary politics for the liberation of all. Instead of challenging the disciplinary constraints that impede a complex historical narrative, one based on a dynamic geographical and temporal context, Marx settled for a detailed narrative of a very little piece of the whole puzzle that is colonialism. What he missed, or intentionally turned away from, was how the imperial state-apparatus managed intellectual property for the purpose of creating technologies to bolster industry. Had he been attuned to this network of the imperial states and the university, he might have seen that what was happening to workers in the space of Europe was a kin, although less violent and torturous, to what was occurring in the colonies. In *Capital*, Marx (1976) writes that there was a

> revolution that took place in the production process at the expense of the workers. *Experimenta in corporevili* [Experiments on a worthless body], like those of anatomists on frogs, were actually being made here ... These experiments were not made just at the expense of the worker's means of subsistence. His five senses also had to pay the penalty. ... But the workers did not just have to suffer from the experiments of the manufacturers inside the mills, and of the municipalities outside, from reduced wages and absence of work, from want and from charity, and from the eulogies uttered in the Lords and Commons. 'Unfortunate females, in consequence of the cotton famine, were at its commencement thrown out of employment, and have thereby become outcasts of society; and now, though trade has revived, and work is plentiful, continue members of that unfortunate class, and are likely to continue so. There are also in the borough more youthful prostitutes than I have known for the last twenty-five years' (586-7).

The Imperial regulation of cotton, its production and exchange, created the conditions for the sexual exploitation of women; the rape and torture of slave women and girls in the colonies and the limiting of economic opportunities of women and girls in the metropole. Moreover, workers in Europe were being subjected to experiments to increase their efficiency and productivity while slaves in Haiti, then called Saint Domingue, were being experimented on to test the veracity and effectiveness of plant poisons;

> Regarding the connection between colonial fears over poisons and this tradition of useful medical research, no ambiguity exists about the last instance, for in 1758 at least, colonial physicians experimented with poisons on human subjects, presumably killing the two condemned slaves put at their disposal (McClellan 2010, 146).

While researchers in one place were collecting data about the limits of the worker's five senses, other researchers were testing the limits of life on captive slaves. Moreover, others were competing for a prestigious prize for the development of technologies and practices to increase the slave's chance at survival during the middle passage;

> The French slave trade was the largest in the world in 1780's, and slavery and the triangular Atlantic slave trade propelled French colonization in the Caribbean and South America. Issues touching on slavery run throughout our narrative, and we are far from writing slavery out of the story. Indeed, official eighteenth-century French universities bolstered slavery and the slave system.
>
> Many telling examples support this unfortunate, but unsurprising fact. The best known is the 1772 prize offered by the Bordeaux Academy for the best means of preserving the health of slaves on the long Middle Passage from Africa to the American colonies. Bordeaux (along with Nantes) was the main center of the French slave trade, so it is no wonder that Bordeaux Academy posed this question and others like it. Scions of the great commercial house in Nantes, the Montaudouin brothers Daniel René (1715-1754) and Jean-Gabriel (1722-1780), were themselves slave merchants who were also elected and active *correspondants* of the Paris Academy of Sciences; Jean-Gabriel was also a property holder in Saint Domingue. Books and dissertations devoted to the health of slaves crop up in the context of the Colonial Machine, such as *Observations sur les Maladies des Nègres*[Observation on the Illnesses of Blacks] published in 1776 by the royal

physician, inspector of colonial hospitals, and *correspondant* of the SociétéRoyale de Médicine, Jean-BarthélemyDazille(McClellan 2011, 34).

What McClellan (2011) exposes is a strategic triangulation between the university, and the imperial state in bolstering and engineering the capitalist slave trade. This is a strategic relation essential to the development of the capitalist mode of production and colonialism in the context of Empire. A relation that Marx misses in his pursuit of an analysis of the commodity form. This is again, not to condemn Marx, but rather to acknowledge this missed opportunity. More importantly, to grieve those times where we fail to see how our histories of oppression, and resistance, are intertwined. This is, as Harvey (2012) suggests, also a moment of possibility; he asks: "So what is it that Marx's political economy can do for us, and what is it that we have to do for ourselves" (5). How can we intervene in Marx's intention, how do we truly begin to account for the complex development of the capitalist mode of production in a way that makes central colonialism?

To make central colonialism is to resist the realist paradigm, to resist the shredding of reality into divergent narratives, to resist how knowledge is produced in the university. Most texts about colonialism do not adequately define or explain colonialism. To write about colonialism is difficult, as its continuity over vast space make such an effort seemingly impossible, which is why so many choose to focus on particular projects or aspects of colonialism. A strategy that Edward W. Said's (1979) did not employ in writing *Orientalism*. While not about colonialism, *Orientalism* has been a central text of studies of coloniality. This is peculiar indeed. Said's (1979) book is a canon for studies of coloniality, but what he discusses is not colonialism per se, that is, how it is generally understood as well as defined. Said is interested in discussing the relationship between Europe and its imagined space to the East. He argues that the "Orient was almost a European invention, and had since antiquity a place of romance, exotic beings, haunting memories and landscapes, remarkable experiences" (Said 1979, 1). The *Orient* is not a place, people, or culture. For Said (1979) this relationship is not descriptive of the *Orient*, but rather, descriptive of a process:

> Orientalism can be discussed and analyzed as the corporate institution for dealing with the Orient- dealing with it by making statements about it, authorizing views of it, describing it, by teaching it, settling it, ruling over it: in short, Orientalism as a Western style for dominating, restructuring, and having authority over the Orient (3).

The central argument is that *Orientalism* is the process by which Europe, since antiquity, has developed processes to wield authority, which it could use to facilitate exploitative projects and policies. The concept of *Orientalism* does not forefront conquest, theft of land, genocide, loss of culture, language, and the subversion of social and legal structures. Therefore is not strictly about colonialism, as colonialism is often conceptualized. *Orientalism* is conceptually unique from standard studies of coloniality because Said's (1979) work is not an exposition of facts detailing *Orientalism* as a historical development in the way historical narratives are normatively written. Facts, as used by Said, are of secondary importance. Said's (1979) central concern is to conceptualize a process. *Orientalism* is a process for the installation and continuity of authority and accumulation. For Said, *Orientalism* is an iteration. As such, his work has been foundational to the study of colonialism. Instead of detailing facts about colonial projects, what Said has done is begin a discussion about the temporality and movement of the colonial iteration.

Said avoids the limitations of the realist paradigm because his storytelling is not centrally dependent on established facts. Moreover, his narrative is unique in that he does not replicate the conventions of the discipline of history by relying on a linear temporality. The tempo of his narrative is not based on direct causality, as most historical narratives are. Dominant historical narratives develop according to a cause and effect relationality where one historical occurrence causes or structures the next historical event. In contrast, Said writes to describe a situation. The strength of his narrative lies in his ability to perceive a situation and communicate his perception. Instead of detailing definite historical events as part of a linear sequence, Said's narrative is a story that develops the complexity of *Orientalism*. In each iteration that Said (1979) diagnoses of *Orientalism*, he offers a deeper understanding of its inception and continuity. In this way, Said (1979) offers an analysis of a static temporality. Said's temporal frame is that of a repetitive cycle, of iteration. This is precisely why Said's work is relevant to scholars of coloniality, regardless of their particular focus; because his work offers insight into the system of authority and accumulation, how these processes echo and spread.

Said's (1979) conceptualization of *Orientalism* addresses similar relations as do studies of coloniality, but develops with complexity; he develops a theory of authority and power, based on nuanced principles while avoiding the limitations of the realist paradigm. His theoretical system is based on a central premise. Said (1979) is interested in the development of authority. He traces the historicity of the authority with which Europe created the *Orient*, but does not write a historical narrative of *Orientalism*. Without offering prescriptive features of *Orientalism*, Said (1979) tells a story of its development, without a frame, without a strict definition. In this way, Said's overall approach to theory is unique. Unlike Said's (1979) *Orientalism*, studies of colonialism tend to have a strict temporal context. For instance, the colonization of Central America began in 1492 and ended with the exile of the Spanish Empire. These temporal schemes are very neat; colonialism began in 1492, ended as a result of independence struggles, which ushered in the era of the postcolonial. Said's storytelling develops a temporal frame that is unique from standard temporalizations of coloniality. His temporal scheme is open; there is no start or end date, but rather a general period that initiated a relation, a relation that has the quality of being cyclical. Its temporality is that of initiation and continuity. His temporal scheme is not linear. It oscillates between periods of initiation and continuity. It is the motion of *Orientalism* that concerns Said (1979); how it is that authority contracts and expands to maintain a relation of power over the *Orient*.

While Said's (1979) *Orientalism* emerges in relation to Foucault poststructuralist conceptualization of power, he resists a complete disregard of the structure of *Orientalism*. Said is

> interested in showing how modern Orientalism ... embodies a systematic discipline of *accumulation*. And far from this being exclusively an intellectual or theoretical feature, it made Orientalism fatally tend towards the systematic accumulation of human beings and territories (Said 123)

It is another point where Said's work is unique critical theory. His work suggests a convergence of the symbolic order and the structures of accumulation. In this way Said's (1979) account of *Orientalism* brings together the symbolic and materialist nuances of the interplay of authority and accumulation.

A poststructuralist account of colonialism can make difficult conceptual convergence as poststructuralism encourages the creation divergent accounts of colonialism that often fail to acknowledge that scholars are discussing the same phenomena. While the tendency to privilege discourse is critical to dominant historical narratives that privilege the study of ideologies of race and conquest, they tend to divert their attention from institutionally structured realities of colonialism. Moreover, in its rejection of master narratives, poststructuralism searches for and idealizes subjective interpretation of dominant narratives. This is a tendency that Craig S. Womack sees as ultimately a tension between poststructuralist accounts of coloniality and Indigenous theory. The tension begins in the context that Bonita Lawrence and Enakshi Dua (2005) address in "Decolonizing Antiracism". While studies in postcoloniality and critical race theory have emerged largely as talking back to the disavowal of colonial relations, racism, and white supremacy, these fields have done so based on the disavowal of Indigenous nations and histories. Lawrence and Dua (2005), in speaking about the literature that encompasses critical race theory, postcolonial theory, and theories of nationalism argue that "this literature shares crucial ontological underpinnings. All of these writers fail to make Indigenous presence and ongoing colonization, particularly in the Americas, foundational to their analyses of race and racism" (127). In other words, the spaces within the university that privilege the study of colonialism, racism and white supremacy do so as a denial of Indigenous presence and experiences of colonialism.

Indigenous peoples and nations are trapped in a moment in these narratives, in the moment of contact where dominant narratives of genocide subsumes Indigenous survival and resistance to colonialism. This erasure is the general rule in the university. It is for this reason that the

> role of history is especially important to this discussion. Native literature has often, either directly or indirectly, claimed the role of telling the truth about history, the Indian side of the story we might say. Naming particular historical events and revaluating them in the light of Indian viewpoints is a central endeavour in Native novels, poems, plays, and the attendant criticism of these works. Postmodern theory, with its problematization of master narratives, and its study of the power structures that undergird them, has both supported Native American counternarratives for their resistance to the official story and expressed a leeriness for them inasmuch as they are rooted in any kind of notion of normative truth claims. Some Native critics are frustrated to find out that just when they might finally have an audience for their side of the story, the non-Indian world has discovered that all are subjective. This might strike some as a little too convenient, another abdication of responsibility- in short, a further manifestation of colonialism (Womack 2008 41).

While poststructuralist approaches to history offer institutional space for Indigenous perspectives of coloniality, it is often problematic space that is being made available. It re-inscribes the marginalization of Indigenous experiences of ongoing colonization. By focusing on the symbolic realm without an analysis of how discourse relates to structures, discourse analysis produces a cacophony of narratives (Byrd 2011); where all narratives have value in the analysis of discursive sites. As Indigenous critiques of colonialism are framed as subjective narratives, a certain irony arises. It is the irony of the ascendance of scholarship within universities that is made possible by colonization of Indigenous nations and traditional territories while Indigenous scholarship is labeled as a subjective interpretation among many.

As a result, instead of a poststructuralist approach there is a return to a more structuralist conceptualization of power to underpin studies of colonialism. That turn tends towards a Marxist analysis. Marx's (1976) critique of political economy represents a major break from economists and historians of Marx's time. Rather than assuming the naturalness of the market and market relations, Marx's analysis sought to critically analyze these taken for granted relations and structures. For Marx (1976) the key to understanding the capitalist mode of production is to understand the commodity form. In *Capital Volume 1* Marx (1976) theorizes the commodity to be "an eternal object, a thing which through its qualities satisfies human needs of whatever kind. The nature of these needs, whether they arise, for example, from the stomach, or the imagination, makes no difference" (125). He believed that the commodity form was the central element of a capitalist society and focused on the material conditions of its production and exchange. Marx's (1976) conceptualization of the commodity-form is a reflection of his mobilization of a theory of metabolism. The commodity-form as theorized by Marx (1976) is the analysis of political economy by way of the paradigm of metabolism, interpreted as circuits. Circuits of input and output follow a cause and effect model of analysis. A circuit functions so long as inputs balance with outputs. If one changes, then it affects the entire circuit. In this way, Marx's conceptualization of circuits is an iteration of the realist paradigm.

For Marx (1976), circuits are the context of the interaction between input and output and are analyzed as the local interaction of matter. If an equilibrium in not maintained in the circuit, it will eventually collapse. Such is the case with Marx's (1976) analysis of capitalist agriculture.

> In the sphere of agriculture, large-scale industry has a more revolutionary effect than elsewhere, for the reason that it annihilates the bulwak of the old society, the 'peasant', and substitutes for him the wage-labourer ... [The capitalist mode of production] disrupts the metabolic interaction between man and the earth, i.e. it prevents the return to the soil of its constituent elements consumed by man in the form of food and clothing; hence it hinders the operation of the eternal natural condition for the lasting fertility of the soil. Thus it destroys at the same time the physical health of the urban worker, and the intellectual life of the rural worker ... all progress in capitalist agriculture is a progress in the art, not only of robbing the worker, but of robbing the soil; all progress towards ruining the more long-lasting sources of fertility ... Capitalist production, therefore, only develops the techniques and the degree of combination of the social process of production by simultaneously undermining the original sources of all wealth- the soil and the worker (637-8).

Marx (1976) argued that capitalist agriculture robbed the soil of its nutrients as the factory robs the worker of his life-force. Capitalist agriculture and production of commodities, for Marx, can be understood as a circuit of input and output. Significantly, for Marx's (1976) analysis of agriculture the soil becomes the research context, and the circuit the analytic site. Marx's (1976) main critique of capitalist agriculture is that in the sole intention of the efficient production of commodities on a large scale, agriculture has developed to maximize harvest yield. The consequence of which leaves the soil eroded of its nutrients. In this analysis, output exceeds input- as early capitalist agriculture did not employ any fertilizers or means of returning nutrients to the soil. Leading to the collapse of nutrient equilibrium, which tended towards the collapse of the system.

For Marx (1976), the site of analysis is the context of commodity production, as such, he is primarily interested in a critique of the capitalist mode of production- such as his critique of capitalist agriculture. Using this as a theoretical paradigm, Marx analysis could emerge as a criticism of the capitalist mode of production whereby the problematic of the capitalism occurs as commodity production exceeds the capabilities of nature and prevents the well being of workers. In this focus, and because of his application of realist principles, Marx details the part while evading the broader, colonial context of colonialism. Agriculture, and the development of botany, are quintessentially colonial projects. However, as Marx relies on the analysis of circuits in a local context, he misses the reason and rationale for that which he criticizes.

In *Capital* Marx (1976) does not explicitly theorize colonial relations. Rather, he reproduces the tenets of realist paradigm and constructs his context to be local and specific. For Marx (1976), the development of the capitalist mode of production can be understood as the development of the production and exchange of commodities in a society based on social production and capitalist appropriation. In other words, capitalism, as defined by Marx (1976), is a system by which capitalists employ workers to transform raw materials using technology into commodities that the capitalists sell for profit. For Marx (1976) the analysis of the capitalist mode of production traces the circulation of the commodity. What happened before or after the commodity's production is omitted in the analysis; which means that the conditions of possibility for the production of the commodity are disavowed as is its consumption. Instead of focusing on colonial relations- for example, the accumulation of raw materials as a condition of possibility for the emergence of the capitalist mode of production- Marx (1976) addresses what he terms *primitive accumulation* as a supplement to his core analysis of capitalism. As Glen Coulthard (2014) explains

> [c]hallenging the idyllic portrayal of capitalism's origin by economists like Adam smith, Marx's chapters on primitive accumulation highlight the gruesome violent nature of the transition from feudal to capitalist social relations in western Europe (with an emphasis on England). Marx's historical excavation of the birth of the capitalist mode of production identifies a host of colonial-like state practices that served to violently strip- through "conquest, enslavement, robbery, murder"- noncapitalist producers, communities, and societies from their means of production and subsistence. In *Capital*

> these formative acts of violent *dispossession* set the stage for the emergence of capitalist accumulation and the reproduction of capitalist relations of production by tearing Indigenous societies, peasants, and other small-scale, self-sufficient agricultural producers from the source of their livelihood- *the land (7).*

For Marx(1976), primitive accumulation is the backdrop to the real story, which is the circulation of the commodity form. Because Marx (1976) was unaware of the ontological basis of the relation between nature and the economy, he could under-theorize what was arguably the essence of the capitalist mode of production- the violent removal of people from the land. When one makes central the disruption of traditional ways of living with the land and the traditional economies that formed from within traditional ontologies and cosmologies, the development of the capitalist mode of production is better understood as a nuanced colonial iteration. As the iteration is the disruption of dynamic time and motion of sacred sciences through the imposition of static processes- such as the continued production and exchange of commodities. Therefore, to use Marxist theory to underpin studies of colonialism, while fruitful, requires a radical appropriation of Marx's text. It is not simply a question of application, or the use of Marxist theory as exposition or explanation. It requires a suspension of Marx's central premises: that the capitalist mode of production developed in local context, under specific relations of the circulation of the commodity.

In attempts to either justify, or expand, Marx's (1976) analysis in *Capital* there has been a desire to prove the applicability of Marxism for understanding colonialism. The general sentiment is that Marx's realist analysis of the capitalist mode of production is accurate. The feeling is that Marx's analysis of one particular local can be supplanted to any other local context. Herein lies both the possibility and challenge of adopting a Marxist analysis in the study of colonialism, as Marx's (1976) analysis both challenges and echoes the realist paradigm. Marx (1976) offers an analysis on the capitalist mode of production as a process that echoes. This is clearly seen in his analysis of capitalist agriculture. Capitalism, for Marx, is an iteration. Its processes function iteratively; capitalism has the same goals and structure in the context of agriculture as it does in the factory. Leading to the idea that the power of capital structures all societies, regardless of their local eccentricities, anywhere where capitalism is involved or has taken root.

Drawing on Marx, Vladimir Ilyich Lenin and Antonio Gramsci in "[t]heir use of 'internal colonialism' articulated the systemic economic and political inequalities that emerged within a state and were used to extract resources from the margins/peripheries/souths to the center/core/norths of a single polity" (Byrd 130). Internal colonialism becomes a supplement to the central analysis, much in the same way as Marx's concept of primitive accumulation. Coloniality is theorized as a state function to make available raw materials, from the peripheries to the core. In this analysis, Marx's premise holds. From this point, Marx's central argument is solidified; raw materials furnish capitalists with the means to produce commodities. Colonialism is reduced to an economic imperative of the capitalist class, facilitated by the state. For Jodi Byrd (2011)

> [w]hat emerges out of this transit of meaning is a colonialist recursive. And it seems, then, that after Lenin and Gramsci, "internal colonialism" as a concept was an also-and that mapped the imperial European projects of colonialism in the Americas back into Europe itself, creating "internal Americas" out of the very hinterlands that provided Europe with the means to colonize the Americas in the first place. It fundamentally acknowledges the colonization of Indigenous peoples at the same time that is disavows that colonization by making economic disparity standing for Indians within the newly analogized frontier mythos of Europe (132).

The concept of "internal colonialism" describes exploitation that capitalism takes hold of. The concept gives the impression that the capitalist mode of production is independent of colonial relations, that if colonialism did not exist, capitalist would simply acquire raw materials elsewhere, by another means. By focusing on the movement of capital, Lenin and Gramsci acknowledge one specific feature colonialism but disavow the totality of colonialism. As their focus is on the capitalist mode of production, they are primarily concerned in the analysis of capitalism's component parts. In particular of the parts that interact locally. Therefore, the concept of internal colonialism is the analysis of raw materials after they arrive and are used in the factory. In their focus, Lenin and Gramsci miss that colonialism is an initiating feature of the capitalist mode of production, and of Europe itself. In other words, Lenin and Gramsci fail to recognize or adequately acknowledge that the concepts of internal colonization and primitive accumulation do have a specific temporality and are not atemporal- as they are theorized. These relations of European plunder of wealth, of conquest, have initiated the availability of capital, which predates the rise of the capitalist mode of production. These relations of European plunder of wealth, of conquest, are formative of both the symbolic order of Europe as well as its structure of imperial states. By focusing on the flows of capital Lenin and Gramsci miss the entire image by focusing on a single stroke of the brush. Lenin and Gramsci's conceptualization of internal colonialism is an attempt to extend Marx's (1976) analysis in *Capital*. This concept is, however, a colonial iteration of specialized knowledge in so far as it analytically structures dynamic life in the motion and temporality of the iteration by applying the same theoretical paradigm to a different context. It is a colonial iteration of specialized knowledge that seeks to underpin an analysis of coloniality with Marx's theory of class dynamics in the colony.

While Marx advances the realist paradigm he also echoes dualistic thinking (hooks). For Marx the fundamental contradiction of the capitalist mode of production is the antagonism between the capitalist class and the proletariat (working) class. In particular, capitalist appropriation of commodities and surplus-value produced by workers. The resolution to this antagonism is for Marx when the proletariat class appropriates the state as the inception of socialism- social production and social appropriation of commodities and surplus-value. In other words, a take over of the means of production and distribution by workers to displace the capitalist class. This is the instance of dualistic thinking that theorizes structures as driven by an absolute enemy and the local as its developmental site. It is a vision of justice based on violence, where the possibility of grief and healing are secondary to the overthrow of capitalists. Alternatively, for Said "as much as the West itself, the Orient is an idea that has a history and a tradition of thought, imagery, and vocabulary that have given it reality and presence in and for the West. The two geographical entities thus support and to an extent reflect each other" (Said 5). The idea of Europe is a reflection of the idea of the Orient. Neither is accurate of the lands, the people, cultures, and societies that they purport to define. It is the same authority that has created the idea of a Europe and the Orient; it is the same authority that created them in opposition to one another. To destroy one is to destroy both, as they co-exist in a relation of dependence. For Said the way forward is though resolution, not destruction.

The idea of Europe as a definite local is an ideological construction made possible by the realist paradigm. It is the realist paradigm that has colonized historical awareness, such as the idea of European history as a distinct narrative. The realist paradigm has achieved this by imposing the principle that matter interacts locally in the present time with a cause and effect relationality. In this paradigm, European history is the narrative of the interactions of matter and discourse in the geography constructed as Europe. Marx adopts this paradigm in his analysis of the capitalist mode of production as the production and exchange of commodities. Lenin and Gramsci inherit this paradigm from Marx and extend it by focusing on the capitalist mode of production without an analysis of how different locals interact dynamically. Marx (1976) continues this paradigm by theorizing social relations as an antagonism of separate configuration of matter (distinct social groups) interacting in a local context. As such, the materialist conception of history is primarily a historiography based in the realist paradigm. In contrast, as Said

(1979) attends to the significance of structure in his focus on accumulation, he does so through storytelling. Said (1979) tells the story of *Orientalism* as an iteration, thereby offering an alternative to the realist paradigm.

The allure of the realist paradigm is a promise of a more objective history. It suggests the possibility of arriving at a version of history independent from the subjective interpretation of the historian. The promise of an objective history has been delivered as the promise of a more truthful history. Objectives that are irrelevant for historian E.P. Thompson. In "Agenda for Radical History" (1994), Thompson argues "[o]ur concern increasingly must be with finding the 'rationality' of social unreason. That is not throwing up one's hands and saying 'anything can happen in history'- but, rather, finding the 'reasons' for social unreason" (362). In other words, our concern must be to understand what passes as reasonable. For the critical historian, the concern is to understand history by avoiding the realist paradigm that far too often lends itself to creating historical ideology rather than a relevant practice of history. To do this, we must understand who we are, who we have been, and who we will be. This is not to suggest an exodus to poststructuralist conceptualization of subjective historical narratives; nor is it a defense of a materialist conceptualization of history that fixes reality. As both historiographies deny personal and collective ability to perceive what is, and its interrelationality to what has been and what will come to be. Moving forward is a simultaneous movement within and beyond- to embolden our awareness, our innate ability to perceive the totality of world relationships.

Chapter Three: Critical historiography

A productive effort in the face of the erasure of colonialism might seek to name how it is that the presuppositions of the discipline of history create particular situations- such as the history of the university- where the colonial context is efficiently disavowed. This can be accomplished by first identifying the presuppositions of the discipline that lead to a problematic understanding of colonialism. Dominant historiographies of colonialism are based on the following presuppositions: that colonialism is 1) exclusive to the colonies; 2) the result of a cohesive European attitude; 3) best understood through the archives of colonial administration; 4) created by the aggression of white Europeans exclusively against people of colour beyond the space of Europe; and 5) a phenomenon that began after the consolidation of European Empires. These beliefs have been established as the standard configuration of colonial relations. This configuration offers readymade answers to essential questions: Where did colonialism take hold? When did colonialism occur? Who were the colonizers and the colonized? What are the most reliable sources for research about colonialism? Why did colonialism happen? The discipline of history offers answers that not only provide an already established context for research, but also structure the ways in which historians conduct research and interpret data. Instead of offering alternative narratives you and I will think through these assumptions and re-imagine what the criteria of the history of the university might or ought to be.

Where?

When we try to understand relations of conquest, plunder, of colonialism answering the question of where is central. Where did these occurrences take place? This is really a question that initiates and structures historical analysis, and ultimately gives shape to the historical narrative. Generally, colonialism is understood as having occurred outside of Europe. So much so that in the context of Britain, historians speak of the expansion of the Roman Empire; the invasion of the Vikings, the takeover of the Germanic Empire; and the creation of Anglo Saxon rule. Never do historians speak of the perennial colonization of Britain. The historical narrative created is that in the space of Britain wars were waged, control seized, territory occupied by settlers, as well as the general theft of resources by the victors. But in the space of Britain, historians do not call it colonialism.

Colonialism happened elsewhere, never in the imagined geo-political space of Europe. For most colonialism occurs in the territory of the colonized, that is, it is a process that establishes and assumes control over colonies. Within this conceptualization of where colonialism occurs there are some who describe the colonies as passive settings, where people are killed and their wealth extracted. In contrast to this, more recent scholarship focuses on the colony as a complex context: "colonial settings are no longer seen as passive environments, but sites for complex interactions of local cultures with exogenous forces that produced a blend of responses" (McClellan 2011, 18). Another approach is to suggest that colonialism occurs as a relation in-between the metropole and the colony. A relation that is based on the control from a major city center that exercises its power over all the colonies within the Empire. In this model everything flows from the peripheries in terms of raw material and precious metals. Yet, even as colonialism is viewed as a relation- Europe is not a space of colonialism.

Europe, as the site of power, as the cultural epicentre of the colonizers, has never been colonized- or so the story goes. It is a story that defies reason. Reason suggests that if we define colonialism as a set of particular occurrences- occupation of traditional territories by a force that exploits and assassinates, rapes, and appropriates traditional knowledge of those who are on their ancestral lands- then whenever or wherever this set of occurrences take place, it is a situation of colonialism. But we are not dealing with reason. We are dealing with ideas and with ideology.

The idea of Europe is that it is a territory with a distinct culture, a history of progress and social enlightenment. This idea of Europe is set in juxtaposition to its colonies, understood as the space of colonialism. In this scheme, the colony is the territory from which raw materials flow as do the colonized Others. In this narrative, we see a significant belief of distinct cultures, where each culture exists in its own space. In other words, a narrative based on the idea of cultural and geographic isolation. For Homi Bhabha (2004), "cultural diversity is also the representation of a radical rhetoric of the separation of totalized cultures that live unsullied by the intertextuality of their historical locations, safe in the utopianism of a myth is memory of a unique collective identity" (50). In Bhabha we find that culture is experienced as a unique identity based on a radical rhetoric of separation. The passage of time, the occurrences of human interaction have no meaning in this experience of culture. What prevails is a logic of separation, a paradigm that creates division as a logical interpretation of reality. It is a logic that transcends the lived reality of culture. The logic of separation structures experienced reality; to the extent that people see culture as separate entities, and therefore, experience themselves as individuals who collectively share a unique culture and space.

When?

The logic of separation has permeated every aspect of the historian's analysis. It structures the temporal scheme of his narrative. In other words, historical narratives are a derivative of how the historian fractures time. For instance, some historians focus on the 15th century as the inception of colonialism of the Americas, thereby privileging the temporality of encounters between European and the 'new world', citing Christopher Columbus' voyage to Turtle Island in 1492. Others focus on the centuries following, citing a later period of heightened interaction of colonial relations; while others highlight modern colonialism. All of which are examples of how historians apply the logic of separation to articulate the periodization of their historical narratives.

A major issue with this idea of an occurrence as being tied to a specific temporality, whether that be a date or period of time, is discussed by Bhabha (2004) and Hans Belting (2011). In discussing the translation movement Belting (2011) suggests a more dynamic concept of time. He explores how in "Andulasia, the coexistence and cohabitation of three cultures during the Middle Ages provided the impetus for translations of many Arabic texts" (Belting 2011, 3). He explains that the temporality of these translations, in particular the extent to which these translated works influenced the development of Art, can not be temporalized; the temporality of the cultural a/effect of these translations cannot be given a time frame. He explains that some discernable a/effects, such as in the work of Copernicus, are evidenced in what he created. However, it is impossible to know when he had access to translated texts, what period of time it took him to read them, and significantly, the temporality of their creative, intellectual and epistemological influence. There exists an unknowable dynamic of time in the temporality of translations and the cumulative cultural and intellectual a/effect of those translations (Belting 2011, 3).

Moreover, Bhabha (2004) suggests that events that occur in the space of Europe are given meaning, or shaped, by occurrences in the colonies. As Bhabha (2004) asks, how do we encounter historical narratives about Europe given that these narratives are premised on the fact that colonialism happened elsewhere and never consequently in the space of Europe. This is for Bhabha (2004) an ethnocentric limitation to understand the ideological creation of modernity as inherently European. It is a limitation that constructs occurrences in the space of Europe as decidedly not subject to an analysis of colonial relations. In contrast, Bhabha (2004) asks what if the

> spatial sign of modernity become[s] immediately apparent if we take our stand, in the immediate postrevolutionary period, in San Domingo with the Black Jacobins, rather than Paris. What is the 'distance' that constitutes the meaning of the Revolution as sign, the *signifying lag* between event and enunciation, stretches not across the Place de Bastille or the rue des Blancs-Monteaux, but spans the temporal difference of the colonial space? (350).

In essence his is asking about what gives meaning to the French Revolution as a sign of modernity, and suggests that this meaning can be found in San Domingo in the revolutionary movement of the Black Jacobins. For Bhabha (2004) the signifying lag is not only temporal but also spatial. He is effectively questioning how historians construct the matrix of time and space of their historical analysis. Moreover, he suggests that the contextual matrix of linear time and discreet cultures cannot account for the complexity of cultural exchange. Dominant matrices cannot trace where and when cultural exchanges occur, how they a/effected those involved, nor can they define when and where these exchanges manifested in people's thinking, behaviourand politics.

What?

Aside from establishing temporal and spatial matrices that structure historical analysis, the historian must also decide what to analyze. Most commonly, the focus of academic research is based on the analysis of established archives. Archives are documents, artifacts, and data; essentially any form of material culture. At first, this may seem like an extremely reasonable proposition, to analyze material culture of a society or occurrence in order to construct a reasonable historical narrative. It may well be the case, but only if the process of establishing historical archives is first understood as innately politicized. Consider that the creation of an historical archive is the imposition of a worldview as items included in an historical archive are those deemed relevant to the historian. For instance, within the discipline of history, what is often included are written artifacts, to the extent that the archive of writing amassed is perceived to be a legitimate representation of a society or occurrence. This is however a cultural imposition from a society founded on the written word. It is of great significance when historians research cultures that are storytelling, for instance. In the case when a historian looks for written texts, he may be inclined to see a society as nascent or 'primitive' if he cannot find what he values in society- the written word.

Furthermore, Michael Trouillot (1995) argues that the creation of historical archives, while the may give some degree of insight into a society or occurrence, always *Silences the Past*. Trouillot maintains that dominant methods for crafting archives erase particular histories, while they bear witness to others. He explains how the process of collecting material culture is simultaneously a process of exclusion; of disavowal of that which is not viewed as legitimate historical data. Moreover, as McClellan (2010) points out, even in situations where there is an abundant source of what historians view as legitimate archival materials, such as in the case of the development of science in the French colony of Saint Domingue, historians have nearly entirely neglected to recognize or analyze this data (19). McClellan (2010) argues that the reason for this 'oversight' can be found in understanding the French historical consciousness. He suggests that

> to a degree, a recollection of Saint Domingue lingers in the collective memory of the French today. The former colony maintains something of the Wild West, frontier image that it possessed in the eighteenth century, and the character of the rich uncle from the sugar islands has not completely disappeared as a popular stereotype (McClellan 2010, 15).

Leading to the situation where the history of Haiti is disavowed. It is believed to be irrelevant because of the way in which the idea of Saint Domingue lingers in the collective imagination. Haiti, as a sovereign nation, has not materialized in the French historical consciousness. It remains trapped in the colonial imaginary of the French people. Because of this attitude the history of Haiti, its significance to France, is simply not acknowledged. There develops a historical amnesia of the significance in the development in French botany, medicine, and science (McClellan 2010), as well as ideas of liberty, justice and fraternity (Bhabha 2004). When historical archives are amassed they 1) create a particular image of a society or occurrences; 2) erase Other societies and occurrence; and 3) ignore all else.

In this light it becomes significant to understand the nature and quality of historical archives. The dominant belief is that archival materials, while imperfect, provide the best way to understand the history of a society or occurrence. This belief is substantiated by the desire to understand the past coupled with the lack of being able to conduct legitimate historical research otherwise. However, Walter Benjamin (1968) warns against this desire to believe that archival materials describe the past in a straightforward way. Benjamin (1968) argues that for the historian archival materials

> without exception the cultural treasures he surveys have an origin which he cannot contemplate without horror. They owe their existence not only to the efforts of the great minds and talents who have created them, but also to the anonymous toil of their contemporaries. There is no document of civilization which is not at the same time a document of barbarism. And just as such a document is not free of barbarism, barbarism taints also the manner in which it was transmitted from one owner to another. A historical materialist therefore dissociates himself from it as far as possible. He regards it as his task to brush history against the grain (256-257).

In reading against the grain, the historian must, at least to some extent, ignore that cultural artifacts are at once artifacts of conquest. The historian who analyzes archival materials as representative of a society or occurrence must distance himself from the fact of conquest. When he treats archival material as a good measure of culture, he ignores how it has likely made its way to him by way of conquest, and embedded therein are histories erased, peoples assassinated and knowledge/wealth appropriated.

Why?

Despite this tendency to ignore the embedded histories of conquest and plunder in historical archives, there is at the same time an impulse to describe the motivation of people and societies in historical narratives. When discussing European conquest and plunder, historians offer a host of reasons- speculating as to the motivation for violence. A prominent belief is that the impetus for European colonialism was economic; in other words, colonialism is the expansion of mercantilism[4]. Colonialism in this point of view is simply the search for new markets to trade with or simply acquire raw materials and precious minerals under the protection of Empire. Another similar explanation as to why Europeans colonized is that McClellan (2010) calls the drumbeat of utility. McClellan (2010) critiques how for many historians the motivation for colonialism was the

> concept of the useful application of science [which] provides a principal point of departure for understanding the connections between science and colonial development in Saint Domingue: the drumbeat of utility... French science received support because of the many practical benefits it offered or seemed to offer in establishing, maintaining, and enlarging French Saint Domingue. Science could investigate causes of tropical diseases, determine Saint Domingue's precise location, identify useful flora and fauna, and explore potential new avenues for colonial development, particularly promising economic enterprises. The full armamentarium of French science was constantly, relentlessly employed for its real or perceived utility across a broad range of activities (8).

Colonialism was a means to achieve political ends. It is believed that the horrors of colonialism were justified as a 'necessary evil' to acquire what the state and its citizens needed and what would advance the humanitarian development of medicines or science. The terror and trauma of colonialism were justifiable collateral damage. In this scenario, the horrors of colonialism were incidental, not part and parcel of the colonial project.

Another reason described by historians was that Europeans believed in their innate superiority. A superiority premised on the idea that European culture, social structure and spirituality were ideal. Therefore, when they encountered different societies, they had a tendency to construct those peoples as inherently inferior and non-human. Some, who share similar cultural, social or spiritual

---

[4]Mercantilism is "the economic theory that trade generates wealth and is stimulated by the accumulation of profitable balances, which a government should encourage by means of protectionism" ("mercantilism". The Canadia Oxford Dictionary. Ed. Barber, Katherine. :Oxford University Press, 2004. Oxford Reference. 2005).

beliefs were deemed less than. Others, whose societies were unique, and therefore different that those of Europe, were often demonized, going so far as to consider these peoples as sub-human. European culture, set as an idealized norm, led to the hierarchal classification of human beings, which served as the ideological justification for colonialism, for conquest and plunder.

In this understanding of European racism and ethnocentrism, there is a tendency to analyze colonial relations along racial divides. In other words, historians (and social scientists generally) tend to identify the colonizer as white and the colonized as people of colour. In response to this tendency, hooks (2013) offers a nuanced approach to understand the racialization of colonialism. hooks (2013) suggests that it is not simply that colonizers are white that should be the object of study, but rather, the ways in which particular peoples were mobilized based on a shared idea of membership is what is perceived to be a superior race.

> Bonding on the basis of shared whiteness provides the foundation for a sense of shared meaning, values, and purpose. With the battle cry of preserving whiteness, imperialist colonization became the belief system that supported the mass murder of indigenous natives, the blatant stealing of their lands, and the creation of segregated reservations. Despite the presence of African individuals who came to the so-called new world before Columbus- as documented in Ivan Van Sertima's seminal work *They Came Before Columbus*- white supremacists thinking and action condoned the enslavement of black Africans, supporting their brutal exploitation and oppression (hooks 2013, 4).

For hooks, it is significant to name and understand the ideology of white supremacy, it logics and aesthetics, not as a physical embodiment, but rather as a social process that is mobilized within a particular context for specific reasons.

Who?

In dominant histories of conquest and plunder, of colonialism it is white people who are the conquerors, plunderers and colonizers. Within this narrative, people of colour are the conquered, the plundered, the colonized. However, people of colour have also conquered, plundered, and occupied territory that was not of their ancestors. For example, the translation movement, so critical to the development of the university and European culture broadly, was, as Lyons (2009) argues, in part due to Muslim imperialism. Lyons (2009) argues

> Muslim conquest and empire building also restored ancient ties among historic centers of civilization across a huge landmass. This created an invaluable melting pot for intellectual traditions that had been forcibly kept apart for centuries by political divisions: Hellenistic learning that evolved in Greece and, later, Alexandria, on the one hand, and Sumerian, Persian, and Indian wisdom, on the other (57).

Obviously this occurrence of conquest the conquerors were not white, yet it was decidedly a situation of conquest. This is also not a unique example, which points to a serious problematic of white vs. non-white paradigm in historical thinking. This tendency in the discipline is to recount history along the divide of race is not only inaccurate, but problematic.

It is problematic, firstly because it fails to acknowledge that 'race' is a social construct that has no biological basis. When 'race' is mobilized as a basis for historical analysis, historians erase the history of the development of the idea of 'race'. They ignore that the "idea of 'race' is surely the most efficient instrument of social domination" (Quijano 2007, 45). Anibal Quijano (2007) finds it problematic when historians ignore that our modern conceptualization of 'race' emerged during the colonization of the Americas and therefore, was not the reason or rationale for colonization of the Americas. 'Race' was not, at its inception in the Americas, a term with specific reference to skin colour or family descent. Rather, it was used to create specific ideal of cultural hierarchy. Furthermore, Quijano (2007) recounts another meaning within the Spanish Empire;

> The idea of 'race' was born with 'America'; it originally referred to the differences between 'Indians' and their conquerors (principally Castilian). The first conquered peoples to whom future Europeans applied the idea of 'color' are not, however,

> 'Indians'. They are the slaves who were kidnapped and sold from the coasts of what is now known as Africa, and who they called 'blacks [Negroes],' But, surprising as this may now seem, Africans were not the first peoples to whom the idea of 'race' was applied- even though the future Europeans were acquainted with them long before they arrived on the coasts of the future America.
>
> During the Conquest, the Iberians- Portuguese and Castilian - used the term 'black,' a color, as shown in the documents of that period. But the Iberians of that time did not yet identify themselves as 'white.' This 'color' was not constructed until the 18th century, among the Anglo-Americans, as their institutionalized the slave status of Africans in North America and the Antilles. Here, obviously, "white" is the constructed identity of the dominators, counterposed to "black" ("Negro or "nigger"), the identity of the dominated, as "racial" classification is already clearly consolidated and "naturalized" for all the colonizers, and ever, perhaps, among some of the colonized (Quijano 50).

'Race' was differently constituted by different Empires. Quijano (2007) stresses that these racial demarcations signaled an economic structure and not merely an ideological manipulation. Moreover, these definitions changed over time. Eventually, Indigenous peoples became Native, and Africans Black. In the context of the Americas, Europeans eventually became exclusively white simultaneously becoming Creole in the context of Empire. In the colonies they were the epitome of white, of the European culture. In the context of Empire, Creoles were tainted by their quotidian proximity to Natives and Blacks. Thus, creoles became an inferior kind of white.

In dominant historical narratives, white has become a social marker, it is a designation of a particular social group based on the ideology of shared descent. A belief that erases the different constructions of whiteness across Empire in the colonization of the Americas. Furthermore, this belief erases how people who are classified as white do not share a common descent and whose nations have differential historical relations to Empire. In his research, John M. MacKenzie (2008) challenges the idea of a monolithic white, and argues for a complex understanding of descent in spaces defined as white spaces. He looks in particular at the history of war in Britain. MacKenzie (2008) is contesting dominant historiography that characterizes English civil wars as a contestation between kingdoms and armies. For MacKenzie (2008)

> despite this recognition of stresses and strains in the British state, conventional British imperial history took little or no notice of the possibility of a fully interactive approach to the relationships between empire and the various ethnicities of the United Kingdom. Indeed for a long time, the 'domestic' history of Britain was written largely without reference to Empire, except perhaps with regard to some aspects of economic history (1246).

For Mackenzie (2008), the ease with which historians make irrelevant or ignore internal tensions within Britain is problematic. Specifically, historical analysis occurs based on the assumption of a racially or culturally homogeneous Britain prior to the arrival of people of colour in the post-industrial era. Mackenzie (2008) further argues

> within the Empire itself, although there were many scattered references to a variety of white ethnicities, there had been no attempt to examine in any systematic way the manner in which imperial rule had been influenced by the local practices, intellectual or religious traditions of the constituent parts of Britain. The supposition seemed to be that Empire was a solvent not a separator, that British imperial endeavour and the development of the eighteenth-century British nation ('Britons') in the face of its French 'Other' had indeed served to suppress key aspects of individual ethnic histories (1246).

MacKenzie (2008) points out that white as not a singular category in Britain, but rather, there was a complex social organization of people of differential descent, who identified accordingly. Therefore, it is more appropriate to discuss the construction of a complex idea of whiteness that has over time, erased ideas of heterogeneity in descent and supplanted for it an idea of a homogeneous white.

The reality of which is not insignificant. Take for instance the Irish potato famine (1845-1849), which killed over one million Irish people (Woodham-Smith 1962). The potato became an essential staple of the Irish diet given the high price of other staple grains and crops. When famine hit, the state refused to feed the Irish peasants and also refused to interfere with the 'free' market. We have in this example a situation where the infrastructure of international states; 1) in the colonization of the Inca Empire ideas of the racial superiority were mobilized for conquest, genocide and plunder, which included the plunder and colonization of the potato; and 2) in England used the technology of the potato, and crops in general, to create a state of dependency of Irish peasants, who were seen as a inferior type of white. The infrastructure of international states continued the colonization of the Irish by using the means made available through the colonization of the Inca, administered by an international network of Empires.

PART FOUR:
Iterations of history

Systemically, colonialism is a multiplicity of iterations. In the context of the university, the multiplicity of colonial iterations has structured knowledge. At the level of the university this has been accomplished by the institutionalization of the realist paradigm. From within the realist paradigm facts become quantifiable configurations of matter. Facts become unhinged from the theorist and reality. As these facts are institutionally mobilized, structured knowledge is institutionalized. The realist paradigm mobilized in subsequent embedded contexts of the university- such as disciplines- forms new colonial iterations that continue to structure knowledge. Colonial iterations in the university construct awareness of reality as knowledge of facts. In this way, awareness of reality is no longer experienced as the perception of a situation. The structuring of knowledge through the realist paradigm has created a situation where colonialism is known, yet the totality of colonialism as a social situation is not fully perceived or understood. Colonialism, as an iterative process, alters awareness by controlling the perception of reality.

Colonial iterations establish narratives of ideal social life, which serve to disavow the reality of colonialism and normalize colonial projects. Social relations are controlled by structuring them to resonate with dominant narratives, by making the realist paradigm the norm. Knowledge as defined by the realist paradigm is the only legitimate knowledge. Dynamic time and movement are erased. Dynamic time and movement, from within the realist paradigm, are not real and therefore, cannot be mobilized to describe reality. In this way, the creation of dominant narratives serves to structure perception. Perception, in tune with dominant narratives, facilitates the continuity of colonial projects. Perceiving realistically is essential to the colonial iteration, as it is a process for the implementation of imperial time and space. The outcome of this process is that social life is spatialized and temporalized to become static. Static life is living in the colonial iterative, of living in accordance to dominant narratives of social life that prescribe the end of colonialism, even as colonial projects continue. The structuring of the status of knowledge and perception have the consequence of altering awareness and life. This is the current motion of colonialism, a iteration of the spectacle that conceals its continuity.

To describe colonialism as the transformation of dynamic life into iterative cycles is to discuss patterns, not development. Life develops, colonialism is a pattern of control. The culmination of colonial iterations becomes prescriptive of reality. As a result, reality is manipulated to develop in relation to this prescription. While the iterations remain static, they simultaneously manifest diversely. The patterns of diverse manifestations of colonial iterations involve three interrelated components. In a historiography, colonial iterations 1) establish an ideal narrative that 2) disavows colonial relations while 3) concealing its continuity. Knowledge becomes empirical and objective in the colonial iterative. Knowledge is established as that which is tangible, quantifiable by measurements of matter. In the realist paradigm, colonialism becomes the history of the colonies. In this becoming there is a simultaneous creation of an institutional structure of disavowal. Colonialism becomes the study of occurrences in the colony, occurrences that are tangible and quantifiable. In this paradigm, dynamic time and movement are made illusive

In the colonial iteration knowledge created is impersonal and experienced as an externality, an abstraction. Abstract knowledge is more readily believed than intimate perception. In the abstract, facts become solidified truth. Conversely, intimate perception of reality is suspect. The subjective quality of intimate perception suggests that this way of knowing is of limited significance. In contrast, knowledge of facts is deemed objective and of great significance. Leading to a situation where knowledge formed as part of a colonial iteration is more readily believed than one's perception.

Each colonial iteration makes the study of the totality of colonialism illusive. The university and its relation to colonialism is made illusive by the dominant narrative of the history of the university. The dominant narrative of the history of the university is of the university as a uniquely European phenomenon. The colonial iterative in the context of the university creates a narrative of the university that conceals its relation to colonialism. The colonial iteration constructs knowledge in such a way that the study of colonialism and the study of the university rarely coincide. To the extent that the university is believed to be the site for analysis of colonialism instead of an institution of colonialism. Iterations of colonialism are simultaneously templates that configure time and space to fit the logic of separation and create discourses that consolidate local space and time as the parameters for research. In the discipline of history historical relations are studied in a local context in linear time. The study of history becomes the study of archives and material culture in the location of their materialization. In this way, the practice of history has developed to conceal the long standing relation between the university and Empire. The discipline itself has developed to conceal the role of Empire in the development of the university.

In the discipline of history we see a tendency to define colonialism in its specificities, often moving away from describing colonialism generally. In the search for specificity, what is lost are the large scale projects of the international infrastructure of imperial states that span extensive time frames. Henceforth, a decolonizing historiography includes an analysis of imperial state projects that occur over complex geographic and temporal contexts. By focusing on the Imperial state-apparatus we can see how its projects occur simultaneously in different spaces, while they differentiate in their specificity, they are nonetheless authored by the imperial state. One such project is the control of intellectual property. When we shift our analysis to the state administration of knowledge production and control of intellectual property, what emerges is a history of the university as an institution of Imperial states.

Chapter Four: A critical precedent

Dominant narratives about colonialism all address occurrences of genocide, the expropriation of raw materials and wealth, as well as theft of land. Rarely does the appropriation of knowledge make the list. In part due to the fact that history is often the stories of kings and their wars. This is, as the story goes, the stuff history is made of. Rarely does one read history books on ancient wars and think that it directly relates to them, especially those of us undertaking the task of higher learning. Dominant histories of the university narrate that the university is uniquely European. Within this dominant narrative, the inception of much of the European intellectual tradition originates in Ancient Greece. In this origin narrative of the canon, Aristotle is a key founder of European intellectual life. This dominant narrative erases the appropriation of knowledge through colonialism; an erasure that disavows the relation between colonialism and the foundation of the European canon. It also obscures the ways in which colonialism is a condition of possibility for the emergence of the university and innovation in intellectual life and knowledge production. An analysis of alternative narratives implicates the university in the appropriation of the Other's knowledge in European universities. Instead of the history of kings and their wars, a focus on coloniality uncovers how plunder and the appropriation of knowledge are technologies of Empire where the university served as the site of conversion, from colonial stolen wealth into intellectual capital.

Colonialism forms the foundation of the European university by way of an iterative relation rooted in Ancient Greece through the relationship between Aristotle and Alexander. In particular, this foundation of the coloniality of the university has its inception in the king's right to plunder. The right to plunder that initiates this alternative narrative of the European university's implication in colonization begins with Alexander of Ancient Greece, in particular, Alexander's wars of destruction. These wars were Panhellenic wars against the *Orient*, the imagined space of barbarity. The atmosphere that Alexander was raised in was his father warring with the Persians and his tutor, Aristotle enraged by the abduction and torture of his father-in-law (Tierney 1942, 226). In 341 B.C. Aristotle's father-in-law was kidnapped and tortured in Susa in an attempt to reveal King Phillip's II plan. Furthermore, as Aristotle's instruction centered the work of Homer, Alexander grew up believing that he was the descendent of Achilles and Hercules (Tierney 1942, 226). Therefore, in his conquest of Asia, Alexander saw himself as the avenger of Greece (Ibid). Aristotle's and Alexander's relation grew from and extended an anti-Asian xenophobia. Alexander's wars centered "destruction [which] was at once an act of terror and vengeance. The message was unmistakable: more than a mere punitive expedition, this was to be a war of conquest, and it was to be a Panhellenic effort" (Heckel and Tritle 2011, 96-7). Alexander's conquest was ideological and material. Ideologically, Alexander's war was a demonstrative project with the intention to solidify a Panhellenic identity. This identity was to be defined in contradistinction to its Other. In other words, Alexander's war was a crucial element in the development of *Orientalism*, in the co-creation of the imagined spaces of Europe and the Orient. To be Hellenic was not to be 'Oriental'. Such a proposition required a material base, in the form of destruction and terror. The ideological construction of a Hellenic identity as a propaganda campaign required a demonstration of this destruction.

> Greek allies, mindful of the League's propaganda, demanded the destruction of the city in hope of sating their hunger for revenge and boot. Victorious and laden with spoils, they expected to be demobilized. To deny the soldiers of League, as well as his Macedonian veterans, the right to plunder would be a failure to acknowledge their sacrifices, but Parmenion rightly advised that Alexander should not destroy what was now his (Arr. 3.18.11). Hence the king compromised, allowing his troops to pillage while still reserving the greatest treasures for himself; for even in the suburbs there were enough spoils to go around. But, if the destruction of the palace was an act of policy, it was an unfortunate miscalculation. Alexander may have attempted to limit the physical destruction while satisfying

the expectations of the Greeks back home; the symbolism of the act was, however, seared into the hearts of Iranians for centuries (Heckel and Tritle 2011, 99-100).

Alexander's wars fueled the creation of a Greek identity in contradistinction to the *Orient*. The right to plunder was part and parcel of the creation of this identity, as the Greeks believed that their victory gave them the right to take what they pleased and destroy the rest.

This occurrence of conquest and plunder were no trivial matter. They signaled the horrible violence survived by the Persian Empire and the simultaneous elevation of Europe. As Dimitri Gutas details "all sciences began in Persia and [those] sciences were translated into Greek at the time of Alexander's invasion of Persia, thus leaving the Persians deprived of their legacy after the cataclysmic devastation that befell then at the hands of Alexander" (quoted in Saliba 2007, 11). Alexander's war, his conquest and plunder, in addition to the plunder of wealth and material goods, was an active appropriation of knowledge. Knowledge that became formative of one of the greatest philosopher's of Ancient Greece, Aristotle, who subsequently influenced what is considered to be the one of the foundational sources of European knowledge. Alexander's solidification of a Panhellenic identity has been the root of European identity. Moreover, the appropriation of Persian sciences and philosophy became part of Europe's unique development in philosophy and science.

The canon of what has been constructed as European philosophy and science has its mythical origin partly in Ancient Greece. Dominant narratives of the development of science tend to emphasize its foundation in ancient Greece (Lloyd 1970, 1); which is distinct from Gutas' narrative. In question is what Alexander did with his plunder, in particular, the knowledge he appropriated. This is a question of some significance considering that dominant narratives of the development of European philosophy and science ignore and silence Alexander's plunder of knowledge. This silencing of Alexander's plunder by some is insignificant as they perhaps believe that his appropriation of knowledge is unrelated to the development of philosophy and science in Ancient Greece. They may believe that Greek philosophy and science were so highly developed that the knowledge that Alexander appropriated was of little consequence to Greek scholars. This belief is however incorrect. During Alexander's time Greek science was not comparable to Persian science. Persian science, in particular mathematics and astronomy, developed out of Babylon science where "Babylonians far surpassed the Egyptians in both mathematics and astronomy" (Lloyd 1970, 6). Alexander's appropriation of Persian knowledge, in the name of Greece during the formation of a Panhellenic identity, was the appropriation of knowledge that far surpassed Greek scholarship. This appropriation of the Other's knowledge led to "[g]reat advances in science, especially in geographic knowledge, [which] were made as a result of Alexander's campaigns, and that they were possible is unquestionably due to Aristotle" (Tierney 1942, 226). In their relationship, that of Alexander and Aristotle, we see the development of "this Hellenistic pursuit of science [to which] we owe a great part of [European] civilization" (Ibid.). In this alternative narrative, proposed by Gutas and Tierney, we find a distinct history of knowledge production in Ancient Greece, knowledge that was to become the canon of disciplined learning. Both Gutas and Tierney point to how Greek philosophy and science were significantly and irrevocable enriched by the appropriation of Persian knowledge.

The appropriation of superior knowledge was worthwhile for a people who valued and made use of intellectual innovation. Alexander's conquest included the large-scale plunder and appropriation of Persian and Babylonian knowledge, the significance of which is attested to in one of Europe's most celebrated and studies texts, Plato's *The Laws*. As an appendix to *The Laws* Epinomis writes that in

> this treatise it is conceded that the Greeks, owing to their geographic position, have been later than the Orientals (by which is meant the Babylonians and Persians) in reaching knowledge of the divinity of stars. The hope is then expressed

that soon, "under the guidance of education, of the Delphic Oracle, and of the legalised forms of worship," the Greeks will surpass their barbarian teachers in the practice of the new religion (Tierney 1942, 224-5).

In appropriating Persian and Babylonian science, mathematics and astronomy Greek scholars were exposed to knowledge and ways of knowing that were acknowledged to be superior to their own. It is clear in Epinomis' writing that although he conceded the superiority of Persian and Babylonian sciences, he did so with contempt. It is precisely this scenario that has created the European canon, the simultaneous appropriation of what is acknowledged to be superior knowledge and construction of the Other's inferiority through an attitude of contempt.

Significantly, Saliba (2007) argues that all knowledge production requires a supportive social infrastructure. He argues that a society must have the means to support intellectual development. In general, knowledge production is the result of infrastructure supported by 1) the social desire to learn; 2) an existent knowledge base from which to conduct research; and lastly 3) the infrastructure to support researchers and educators. In Greece this infrastructure was enriched by conquest and plunder. Significant intellectual innovation in the university occurred as a direct result of colonialism. At significant moments of intellectual innovation Europe lacked the social infrastructure needed to independently create these innovations in knowledge production.

Alternative narratives focus on this relationship between the conditions of possibility for knowledge production and the appropriation of the Other's knowledge in Europe. These alternative narratives argue that the appropriation of the Other's knowledge is a condition of possibility for knowledge innovation. In this context, the university is the site for the conversion from colonial plunder to imperial capital. A relation which is rooted in Greece, in particular, in that Aristotle's philosophy that emerged in relation to Alexander's conquest and plunder- and not only Aristotle. Aristotle's appropriated of Persian philosophy and science, an appropriation that has been concealed in dominant narratives about Ancient Greece as the foundation of European intellectual life. Suggesting that Ancient Greek philosophy and science were not entirely Greek. Tierney (1942) writes that

> Under the influence of perhaps of Aristotle's friend, Eudoxus of Cridus- probably, next to himself, the most brilliant thinker among Plato's associates- the Academy had for years before the master's death taken a great interest in Oriental science and religion. The interest produced some remarkable results.
>
> Eudoxus seems to have been not only a close student of Babylonian astronomy and cosmology but also to have had a real knowledge of Zoroastrianism. There is no doubt but that this knowledge was shared by Plato and that it has left traces in his later dialogues, especially in the *Laws* (224).

From Plato to Aristotle, Greek philosophy and sciences developed in relation to the study of 'Oriental' science, mathematics and philosophy.

For instance, Aristotle's work was shaped, enhanced or made possible by Alexander's plunderasthe Greek knowledge base was insufficient to account for the intellectual innovations made by Aristotle. In his story, Abu Sahl b. Nawbakht writes the following:

> The kinds of sciences from which the science of the stars takes its indication of future things were already known and described in the books of the Babylonians. It was from those books that the Egyptians had learned their craft, and the Indians have also employed it in their own country. That was at the time when those ancient people had not yet committed sins and evil deeds, and had not yet sunk as deeply into the ignorance that caused their minds to become confused and their dreams to abandon them. Their confusion led to the loss of their religion, and thus they became totally lost and completely ignorant. They remained in that condition for a while until some of their descendants experiences an awakening that allowed them to remember the past sciences and the conditions of bygone days and how things used to be governed and consequences used to be drawn about the state of the inhabitants and the positions of their celestial spheres, their paths, and their details as well as their celestial and earthly mansions in all of their directions. That happened at the time of the king Jam son Ūnjihān the king.

> The learned from among the people knew those things at that time and recorded them in their books and explained the contents of those books. They described, as well, the conditions of the surrounding universe in all its majesty and the causes of its foundation and its stars (Saliba 2007, 31).

From this passage we can ascertain that Babylonian astronomy was well developed and their understanding of time was complex. In contrast, Greek astronomy was nascent, and their conceptualization of time less developed. As Momigiano explains the "Greeks conceived times as a cycle" (4), developing by way of the motion of a circle's path (5). As "Greek knowledge is based on the eye" their understanding of time was based on their study of the natural world (Ibid.). In contrast, the Persians and Babylonians were charting the universe, and thus developed a complex idea of time, which took into account the universal motion of the planets and star configurations whereas Greek conceptualization of time followed natural cycles observable by the naked eye.

However, the same cannot be said of Aristotle's conceptualization of time. Ursula Coope (2005) argues that Aristotle saw time as a 'universal order' (5). Coope (2005) explains that the questions that Aristotle asks are not ones that follow the types of questions being asked by contemporary philosophers (4). Aristotle's conceptualization of time is unique and nuanced. As Coope (2005) describes, Aristotle's idea of time is closely tied to change. In Hellenistic thought, based on the study of nature, cyclical time is the context of change. However, for Aristotle, change has no reference of time (Coope 2005, 1). Furthermore,

> Aristotle assumes that change is, in an important sense, prior to time. Time is something that is essentially dependent on change, and because of this, a true understanding of time must draw upon a prior understanding of change. This implies that change itself can be defined in a way that makes no reference to time. It thus rules out a certain natural way of using the notion of time to define change (Coope 2005, 5-6).

Aristotle's conceptualization of time was not Greek. It is more nuanced than the knowledge base of the Greek tradition of his time; it extends beyond the cyclical patterns of change of the natural world. In abu Sahl b. Nawbakht's story we see that Babylonian science was closely tied to the idea of change and time as having a complex relation, in so far as astronomy was used as a tool of prognosis. Moreover, the Babylonian idea of change is different from Aristotle's, who believed that change had no reference to time (1). Therefore, Aristotle's conceptualization is not strictly an imitation of Babylonian science; nor was it derivative of the knowledge base of Greek science or his contemporaries.

The conditions of possibility (Saliba 2007) for the emergence of Aristotle's work included Aristotle's relationship with Alexander and in particular the social and cultural infrastructure made possible by colonialism. To explain this occurrence we have two oppositional historical narratives. The dominant narrative suggests that this occurrences is of little significance where the appearance of this knowledge is stripped of it relation to colonialism, to conquest and plunder. Rarely- if ever- in the dominant narratives do historians acknowledge how this knowledge was appropriated, much less that it shaped the development of what was to become the European intellectual canon. Recently, through alternative narratives of the appropriation of African, Arabic and Indigenous knowledge are counter-narratives that center colonialism. They subvert and call into question the idea of Europe; they suggest that if it were not for the violent appropriation of the Other's science and philosophy, Europe would have developed in ignorance and its greatest intellectual and social achievements would never have come to be. These new historians ask us to end the disavowal of colonialism in the history of Europe. They ask that we let go of the lore of Europe, that we acknowledge European conquest and plunder, and understand the ways in which the appropriation of the Other's knowledge was key to the development of European intellectual as well as the university.

Saliba (2007) explains that knowledge was shared, expanded upon and/or spread across large expanse of territories crossing national boundaries and cultures. And in translation, this knowledge developed and at some point, it can no longer be considered purely Babylonian, or Persian, or Egyptian, or Greek, nor can or should it be attributed to a particular scholar, such as Aristotle. Astronomy- and its complex and nuanced conceptualizations of time- in its movement and translation has been facilitated by a human need/desire to learn and is a human effort. Now, we can perhaps accept this, but what of Alexander's conquest, or his violent plunder? Put another way, how can we understand Aristotle's work as part of a human effort to expand awareness of the universe when he profited and benefitted from conquest and violence? Perhaps if we begin with an understanding of the pursuit of knowledge and its relation to conquest and plunder that includes acknowledging when, and under what conditions, knowledge is appropriated and mobilized.

In trying to understand Aristotle, we can look at the concept of *Energeia*, which was a significant intellectual innovation that is unique to Aristotle. Through the concept of *Energeia* Aristotle sought to focus on the "proper work of a thing [its] end" (Bradshaw 2004, 9). He distinguishes two cases to define what he understands to be proper work. In the first case, he distinguishes between a thing and it use (i.e. if a house is the thing, house holding is its use). In the second case, the thing is indistinguishable from its proper work (if vision is the thing, than it is indistinguishable from its proper work of seeing). Through *Energeia* Aristotle was interested in the action as an end, which he conceptualizes as a break from the concept of *Kinēsis*.

Combining these observations from Ethics with those in metaphysics ix 6, we arrive at the following table.

Kinēsis	Energeia
1. Has a termination	1. Has no termination.
2. Is not an end, but is for the sake of an end.	2. Is an end or has an end within it.
3. Complete when it achieves what it aims at, i.e., during whole time or at final moment.	3. Complete at any moment because it does not lack anything which coming into being later will complete its form.
4. Must cease before perfect tense can apply.	4. Present and perfect tense apply simultaneously.
5. Has parts which are different in kind from one another and from the whole; the "whence" and the "whither" give then their form.	5. Homogeneous.
6. Occurs quickly or slowly.	6. Does not occur quickly or slowly.
7. In time.	7. In "the now".

(Bradshaw 2004, 10).

The concept of *Energeia* represents a significant intellectual innovation. It is innovative with respect to contemporaneous understanding of work, in particular, when contrasted to its contemporaneous concept of *Kinēsis*.

The concept of *Energeia* is for David Bradshaw (2004) uniquely Aristotle's. Bradshaw (2004) explains "Aristotle discusses its etymology only once, remarking briefly that *energia* is derived from 'deed' or 'thing done' " (1). Bradshaw (2004) argues that what is significant of *Energeia* is that Aristotle "systematically separated Energeia from its early associations with motion and change" from *Kinēsis* (7). The key distinguishing feature between these concepts is in their distinct conceptualizations of time. In Kinēsis we see a temporal scheme close to what Momigliano refers to as the Greek conceptualization of time. Kinēsis rests on a temporal scheme of cycles, where these cycles are measured by meeting a goal or the completion of an event or end. Kinēsis evolves in time. In contrast, Aristotle's conceptualization of Energeia is based on a multi-temporal scheme, of becoming in the present 'now'. Because it always contains an end, Energeia is constant and for itself. This temporal scheme is not Greek, and is closer to the complex and nuanced understanding of time of Babylonian and Persian astronomy. In Aristotle's conceptualization of *Energeia* we see a significant moment of his intellectual innovation that could have only occurred as a result of Alexander's plunder and appropriation of Persian knowledge.

Despite the significant intellectual innovation Aristotle made in conceptualizing *Enrgeia,* he did not claim it. Perhaps he did not do so because he knew that it was not is to claim. Perhaps he developed this concept as part of his contribution to human knowledge and therefore felt that it was inappropriate to claim an intellectual innovation that did not begin with him, nor would end with him.

> Although Aristotle never takes credit for coining the word *energeia*, there can be little doubt that it was his own invention. It appears nowhere in extant Greek literature prior to Aristotle, and even for some decades after his death it is restricted mainly to philosophical writers, particularly those of Aristotle's own school. By contrast, it occurs 671 times in Aristotle's works, about once for every other page of the Berlin edition (Bradshaw 2004, 1).

For Bradshaw, (2004) Aristotle did not take credit for an accomplishment, which according to Bradshaw (2004), was obviously his to claim. However, it could have been that Aristotle could, or would not, take credit for innovations he knew were not originally or exclusively his own. Perhaps this was a subtle or implicit acknowledgement of his appropriation of Babylonian and Persian knowledge. This is not intended as a project to redeem or vilify Aristotle, as he did appropriate Persian and Babylonian astronomy- - in particular complex and nuanced conceptualizations of time- and did not acknowledge this. Moreover, his hatred contributed to Alexander's conquest and plunder. It is simply a glimpse of what could have been. As Tierney (1942) writes, there was a time where "Aristotle's admiration for Persian religion, which in his case, as in that of Plato, went so far as to suggest an ultimate fusion between the cultures of Persian and Greece" (225). We see that Aristotle's work was on this trajectory; his ability to create a fusion of knowledge systems is precisely what makes Aristotle a unique thinker.

There can be no redemption- that is significant- of Aristotle's politics of knowledge production. He could have, should have, explicitly acknowledged the scholars to which his work was indebted. He could have, should have, spoken out forcefully against the violence that made his work possible, underscoring conquest and plunder as a condition of possible for the innovations of his and others work. This is however, not a persecution of Aristotle. I offer a configuration of this occurrence as a moment of grievability. I grieve the possibility of what could have been the unique pursuit of human knowledge. I also grieve the precedent this set, the normalization of the constellation of knowledge production, complicit scholars and colonialism.

Chapter Five: Technologies of empire

In Marx, instead of a fusion of histories of survival and resistance, we see the continuation of the university's logic. His analysis obscures an understanding of the triangulation of the capitalist mode of production, colonialism and Empire. In Aristotle, instead of a fusion of human knowledge based on mutual respect, we see the inception of a terrible legacy. It is the legacy of the appropriation of African, Arabic, and Indigenous knowledge facilitated by colonialism, conquest and plunder; a legacy crucial to the imperial state. In the process of plunder and appropriation, the imperial state appropriates intellectual property, which through a relationship with universities in Europe, disseminates this knowledge for its own ends. State intellectual property drives ideological and material conditions to strengthen national identity and economic prosperity based on imperial state control and administration of new ideas in the creation of knowledge-based industries and technologies.

Complicit scholars, the university and colonialism

After the fall of the Greek and Roman Empires, Europe fell into what historians refer to as the Dark ages. The science and philosophy of the Greeks and Romans gave way to Christian doctrine coupled with the collapse of virtually all social infrastructure as Europe was torn apart by war, disease, and famine. This was the perfect breeding ground for anti-Asian sentiment, which culminated in a "long and varied history of Christian teachings on permissible war in defense of the faith and the growing popularity of marital metaphors in religious writings eased the way" (Lyons 2009, 12). All of which set the stage for the Christian crusades to the East. As Lyons (2009) narrates

> The warriors of God pushed on to the gates of the Imperial city of Constantinople, their arrival heralded by plague of locusts that destroyed the vines but left the wheat untouched. Their leader, an implacable cleric who had appeared from nowhere to great popular acclaim, exhorted his charges to holy war against the infidel with promises of a home in paradise. Disease and malnutrition were rife. Medical care often involved exorcism or

> the amputation of injured limbs. Torture and other ordeals settled criminal cases.
>
> Few had any learning at all. What education there was back home consisted of memorizing outdated texts under the watchful eyes of hidebound doctors of religion. They had no understanding of basic technology, science, mathematics. They could not date their most important holy days, nor chart the regular movements of the sun, moon, and the planets. They knew nothing of papermaking or the use of lenses and mirrors, and they had no inkling of the prince of contemporary scientific instruments- the astrolabe. Natural phenomena, such as an eclipse of the moon or a sudden change in weather, terrified them. They thought it was black magic (9).

According to Lyons (2009), the state of the *warriors of God* attests to an abandonment of the achievements of the Greeks and Romans in favour of Christian superstition. Lyons (2009) recounts who the crusaders were. From his narrative, it is clear that his purpose is to highlight their lack of knowledge and culture. Lyons' (2009) overall project is to argue that Europe as we know it, as the epicentre of intellect and culture, is in-part the result of the crusaders plunder of Arabic knowledge. Lyons (2009) offers an alternative narrative to the dominant historical narratives of the uniquely European intellectual tradition. His work centers the

> crucial role of the Arabs as master architects- not simply as midwives- of the emerging Western worldview. This was no mere "recovery" of classical wisdom by the medieval Latins, with the Arabs cast in the role of benevolent guardians, as most Western histories of the period tell us. Rather, it represented the enormous transfer- some might even say cultural theft- of invaluable Arab knowledge and technology directly to Christian West (Lyons 2009, 196).

Lyons (2009) narrative contests dominant historical narratives that the appropriation of the Other's knowledge was incidental and its incorporation into European intellectual life was a mark of European innovation and ingenuity. Lyons (2009) is clear that this appropriation was direct, and its effects were that of the profound amelioration of European intellectual life and culture.

After the fall of the Roman Empire, the Dark Ages presented a situation where competing powers sought to take control. One significant player was the Christian church; where the "language of Christian holy war against the Muslim infidel was the perfect vehicle to consolidate church control" (Lyons 50). This language of Christian holy war led to the Crusades and the Spanish inquisition. Spain, Al-Andalus in particular, was a beacon for the Church on the dangers of Arab influence if left unchecked. In southern Spain, the

> Umayyads and their successors produced some of the greatest of the Arab philosophers and scientists, thinkers whose works would one day shake the foundations of Christian Europe. Known among the Arabs as al-Andalus, this region served as an important staging ground for ideas and technology that began to trickle into Western Europe as early as the tenth century (Lyons 2009, 22).

Essentially, the spread of Arabic science and philosophy was a threat to the Church, as it challenged Church doctrine and was attractive to the greatest thinkers of the time who preferred to study with Arab scholars over the monks.

During the middle ages, the Church in an attempt to consolidate control sought to both undermine cities like Al-Andalus, as well as the independent development of university; as both undermined Church doctrine. Some historical narratives of the university suggest that the modern day institution for higher learning emerged in relation to monastic education. However, such narratives fail to mention the presence of Arabic knowledge in Spain and its subsequent spread throughout Europe.

> For their part, most medieval European cities were modest outgrowths of military encampments or ecclesial centers, or congealed gradually around market towns that dotted traditional trade routes. Some grew from settlements dating back to Roman times. But all that changed as the feudal order in the countryside started to unravel, and the peasants fled the land that kept them in bondage to make their own way in the growing urban centers. There they pursued commerce, taking advantage of a general upturn in the European economy driven in part by expanding foreign trade and the emergence of town life. The new urban communes soon organized to defend their

> interests against the nobility, the crown, and the church. Artisans and other professionals founded guilds and corporations to regulate membership, reduce competition, and protect their livelihood. This is the origin of the modern term *university*, which initially described the universe, or totality, or members of a guild or profession. Students and teaching masters who began to meet informally in the towns and cities adopted the institution of the university from the urban guilds; over time, the term's origin became obscured, leaving the word today with the sole meaning of an institution of higher learning (Lyons 2009, 160).

This alternative narrative is one of the emergence of the autonomous university free from the rigidity of Church doctrine and institutional control. For Lyons (2009), the emergence of the university model was very much a movement of the people; organized against the feudal order and the Church, which was dedicated to learning.

The Church implicated in and benefitting from the feudal order saw the rise of these guilds of masters and disciples as a legitimate threat. Although Charle and Verger (1994) minimally address the guild of master as formative of the modern university, they attest to the Church's attempts to seize control of the emerging universities.

> In some cities, there appears what we can call private schools. Teachers set up autonomously and, owing to their reputation alone, taught those who accepted to pay and register with them. In France, these were for the most part based in the liberal arts ... This spontaneous development worried the Church who, since the height of the Middle Ages had affirmed its monopoly in scholarly studies, put into place a system of *licensia docendi*: to open a school, even a private one, from that moment one had to be in possession of an "authorization to teach" delivered by each diocese by Episcopal authority (Charle and Verger 1994, 9; my translation).

The university became the center over the struggle of what was to become legitimate knowledge. Private schools, or the guilds, focused on studying the arts while the Church sought to ensure that learning was to be equated exclusively to the study of theology. In an effort to maintain its monopoly in scholarly studies, the Church instituted the *licensia docendi,* which sought to re-assert the

Church's monopoly of education and what would constitute knowledge by limiting the reach and presence of private institutions and guilds.

At Oxford University, where friars had been welcomed members of the level of masters, beginning in the 13th century, attempted to assert the supremacy of theology and clashed with the university. The secular masters

> insisted that no candidate could be given a license in theology who had not first graduated in arts. The friars, forbidden to study secular subjects, resented this obligation and thought the study of theology should take priority. There were a series of bitter crises. In 1253 Thomas of York, a Franciscan, requested permission to supplicate as a master in theology without having first taken a degree in arts. His supplication was accepted, but the angry regent masters passed a decree that 'no one shall incept in theology unless he has previously inception in arts'.
>
> The dispute was renewed in the early fourteenth century. When, in 1303, the Franciscans were required to fulfil that part of the necessary exercise for the degree, the statutory sermon in St. Mary's Church, they refused, alleging that the church was too noisy. A statute was passed in 1311 insisting that no lectures should be given on the Scriptures before the lecturer had first to lecture for a year on the *Sentences* of Peter Lombard, an obligation resented by the friars. Once more the controversy escalated when a Dominican, Hugh of Sutton, refused to take an oath to observe the statue and was consequently expelled. When the Dominicans secured a favourable ruling from the pope, the university refused to accept it. Eventually an agreement was reached in 1320, largely through the good offices of the archbishop of Canterbury, which left the honours with the secular masters (Green 1974, 12).

Even in the context of co-existence of the friars in the university, the Church intervened, to enter into conflict as to the status of theology in relation to the discipline of the arts. This was a conflict that would take decades to resolve itself at Oxford, which attest to the social power of the Church and the extent to which they saw secular knowledge as a threat.

This conflict between the university and the Church took another character elsewhere than it did at Oxford University. While the friars at Oxford insisted that theology be a standalone field of study, elsewhere there emerged the humanist critique. This would be the most salient and threatening critique to the emerging university. "The most pertinent critiques to the university culture came from humanism. Defied as a movement to reinstate the prestige of the Classics" (Charle and Verger 1994, 33).The humanist critique emerged as a contestation as to what was to be considered legitimate knowledge. With the rise of modern and Arabic philosophy, there was a movement to re-instate the classics (Latin and Greek) and Christian doctrine as the pre-eminent fields of study, and exclusively Western languages as the official languages of higher learning- which was attack against the proliferation of Arabic wisdom in the university. A movement that supplemented Church attempts to maintain its monopoly and emerge as an institutional force.

What we see is the general attempt of the Church to re-assert institutional control of higher learning and what constitutes legitimate knowledge. In the struggle for power that was occurring in Europe, the Church fought the guild of masters, the emerging universities as a means to curb the dissemination of Arabic philosophy and wisdom from cities such as Al-Andalus.

> The translation movement that helped make Michael Scot the leading public intellectual of his day was an export industry, carried out by educated, inquisitive, and independent "knowledge workers" drawn to Spain from foreign lands in pursuit of the *studia Arabum*. The finished goods, in the form of translations, commentaries, and original works, rarely remained behind where they were created. Instead, these were destined for the foreign markets of Italy, France, and England- home to groupings of scholars and students who came together by the early thirteenth century to create the West's earliest universities, in Bologna, Paris, and Oxford (Lyons 2009, 161).

These guilds of learners formed in relation to the translation movement that made Arabic philosophy available throughout Europe, funneled by way of cities such as Al-Andalus. Moreover, the translation movement also re-introduced the works of Greek and

Roman philosophers, whose works had been saved from being obliterated during the Dark Ages. These texts were translated into Arabic, kept safe, and re-introduced to Europe at the cusp of the renaissance. Texts that were not only kept safe during the process of translation, but also ameliorated and augmented by Arabic scholars.

In the context of Europe during the Middle Ages what was at stake was the geo-political structure of Europe. Geo-political supremacy was being fought on the grounds of the universities at Paris, Oxford and Bologna. This was a battle against the culture of learning, of cultural fusion, of cities such as Al-Andalus. Intellectual fusion was taken up by the guild of masters who sought to protect themselves from the union of the Church and the feudal order. Consolidating geo-political power was being largely determined by who could control legitimate knowledge. The ability to define legitimate knowledge in the geo-political space of an emerging Europe would determine control, either by the Church, emerging states or the people. The extent to which the guild of masters and disciples could assert their dedication to Arabic philosophy and science would come shape the character of emerging states.

Both the universities at Paris and Oxford would eventually curb Church control of what would be recognized as the official knowledge- at least to some extent. In the spaces of higher learning, scientism and philosophy would surpass theology in importance for scholarship. However, the humanist critique took hold, as European universities adopted what they saw as uniquely Greek and Roman science and philosophy as central texts of their canon and European languages became the languages of the universities, thereby expelling Arabic and disavowing the significance of the translation movement. While the universities were founded on works created or influenced by African, Arabic, Babylonian and Persian scholars, there was an explicit movement to hide this formation.

What was being hidden, and what was contrary to Church doctrine, was that Arabic knowledge was based on a worldview that harmoniously amalgamated spirituality and science. As a result emerging scholars were being threatened and vilified by the institution of the Church for their preference for Arabic philosophy ad science. Resulting in the separation of modern learning from spirituality and the desacrilization of Arabic knowledge and influence in the university. In the tradition of Islamic knowledge there is a conceptualization of sacred geometry;

> the notion of sacred geometry, measured less by the cartographer's coordinates than by spiritual need or scriptural reading, has long flourished in the human imagination. It contours are shaped by religious experience grafted to common understanding of time and space, rather than by the physical features of the earth or shifting political boundaries of city, state, or nation (Lyons 2009, 80-1).

In the emerging European universities, mathematics was to be stripped of its relation to sacred geometry. European scholars used Arabic mathematics, to a certain extent. Mathematics, as with all the disciplines, would emerge as a standalone field of study, completely separated from the field of theology. The rationale for knowledge production was the separation of the disciplines, and the desacrilization of each discipline. Whereas in the Islamic tradition knowledge production was guided by a spiritual sensibility and moral code, a worldview based on connections, European scholars pursued knowledge within their disciplines based on their personal intentions and within the logic of separation, producing less accurate sciences and temporal awareness.

Prior to the introduction of Persian, Babylonian, and Islamic astronomy and mathematics, European understanding of time lacked the sophistication of their contemporaries. Although Christian temporality was tied to religious time, is so far as it functioned to demarcate prayer time, it was ill equipped to meet basic requirements of tracking the 24 hour cycle of the say. Notwithstanding basic astronomy for keeping time

> [m]ost common of all, perhaps, was the appointment of a senior and respected monk as the *signidicator horarum*, who would chant a set number of psalms to note the progress of the hours and then awaken his brethren for their vigils, to be held at the "eighth hour of darkness." This had the obvious advantage of functioning even when the stars were obscured by the clouds. But the method was so imprecise that theologians were forced to concede that ordinary monks should not be held responsible for any resulting failure by the *significator* to start the required prayer time (Lyons 31).

The significance of Persian, Babylonian, and Islamic astronomy was not only the practical element of keeping time during the day, but also the introduction of a temporal awareness. To be aware of time, for people who had before only had a basic understanding of temporality, was the introduction of a universal awareness; a new consciousness. As Lyons (2009) argues

> Monastic timekeeping, however, was not only a matter for the soul. With no reliable way to measure the passing of the hours, Western man's imagination- and his very existence- remained hostage to the shifting cycles of night and day and the organic phases of planting and harvesting. Accurate timekeeping would one day free society from the dictates of sunrise and sunset and recast the day or the hour as an abstract notion distinct from daily existence. This would eventually foster a new way of looking as the universe as something that could be measured, calculated, and controlled, opening up the realms of science and technology (31-2).

Europeans appropriated this universal consciousness, and with in, the imagination to begin developing philosophy and science more profoundly. However, European scholars did so without the discipline and spiritual awareness of Islamic and Arab scholars and philosophers had in formulating these sciences and knowing.

European appropriation of the Other's knowledge occurred in the context of Alexander and Aristotle's relationship; it occurred in the context of the Crusades; and in the face of Church led attacks against the translation movement. All of these instances of appropriation of knowledge occurred with little regard of the extreme violence peoples faced and continued to live so that this knowledge could take hold- although in a disavowed way. Significantly, this appropriation occurred without any spiritual sentiment, without love, without a commitment to life and reverence for the universe.

The context of the triumph of modern learning over religious doctrine, the desacrilization of knowledge, was an ideal context for the emergence of state intellectual property. After the annexation of Church control of the universities, the state increasingly sought to assert authority over knowledge production.

> At this moment, the interest held by political powers in relation to the universities very well indicated the other major character of the period. While remaining officially institutions of the Church, the universities more and more tendedto fall under the control of cities and of states ... [where the universities] contributed to elaborating a national and monarchic ideology which accompanied the birth of the modern State (Charle and Verger 1994, 19; my translation).

The struggle over universities became a struggle for the emergence and sovereignty of European nation-states. Control over knowledge production in the universities was not incidental, it was crucial for the development of emerging national and monarchic ideologies. Scholars trained at the university went on to fill bureaucratic positions in the state apparatus. In other words, university trained scholars oversaw the ideological and material development of the imperial state within the geo-political space of Empire.

Universities became primary sites for the development of state intellectual property. At Oxford university

> the university enjoyed favour. It was the king who promoted its privileges, protected it against the townsfolk and bestowed his patronage in favour of its clerks. That he should have done this may have represented his belief that it was a royal duty to patronise scholarship; but he realised that Oxford was training the men who were most likely to do him and his kingdom the best service. The university, moreover, promoted the prestige of his kingdom abroad. In the series of disputes which divided the university from the town, the king invariably intervened in favour of the university (Green 1974, 4).

Oxford University came under the protection and direct control of the king. When townspeople repudiated the actions and behaviours of

Oxford scholars, the king seemed to give oxford scholar impunity for criminal and immoral behaviour (Green 1974, 5). Oxford University became a national treasure, a symbol of national prestige. Notwithstanding the significance of Oxford University in the development of British national identity, it was increasing importance in the development of British state intellectual policy. In Britain

> [d]ifferent interests, multiplying as the century proceeded, clamoured for agendas that they wanted the ancient universities to adopt. Governing bodies, professors, tutors, public school teachers, coaches, examiners, Parliamentary Commissioners, graduates, and the public held a variety of views, often conflicting, about the ends higher education should serve. But they all agreed that university teachers must prepare young men for the leadership of church, state and empire. With a clear sense of their mission, Oxford and Cambridge were remarkably successful in turning out graduates who monopolized the dominant positions in public and private life in Britain and throughout the empire (Soffer 1994, 1).

The king's favour was intended to safeguard national and imperial policy in the area of knowledge production. Educating scholars in Britain was simultaneously the training of state and imperial bureaucrats of colonialism.

Moreover, in the king there emerged a national and imperial ruler. His decrees were imperial and national policy administered throughout a state-network encompassing the politically amalgamated territories of the Empire. Although often referred to as European colonialism, with respect to policy and administration, colonialism came under the auspices of the imperial state. This involved the coordination of policies for the appropriation of Indigenous knowledge and development of capacities for knowledge production as well as economic strategies to exploit that knowledge. As Linda Schiebinger and Claudia Swan (2007) argue

> Colonial practices, scientific organizations, and commercial connections differed not only over time but also from place to place: the absolute monarchies of Spain and France operated differently in this regard from the United Provinces of the Netherlands, the constitutional monarchy, or other states (3).

Colonialism was not a monolithic European project; it was differentially implemented by distinct Empires. The king decreed policy to triangulate colonialism, the university, and the economy. Colonialism is thus the structuring of diverse territories guided by knowledge appropriated by university scholars facilitating economic development within the context of Empire. An Empire headed by the king.

It is therefore not difficult to imagine the significance of the king for the Empire. The king, his position in society formed part of a broader cosmology. This cosmology was often based on the belief in the king's divine right to rule, in other words, the authority of the king was God's authority in human relations. It is for the reason that in France, "the king's body and French lands were symbolically aligned in the propaganda and political rituals of the period" (Mukerji 2007, 26). These political rituals can be seen as a cosmology, in so far as they were emblematic of the ways in which people understood themselves in relation to the universe. The king had divine authority, and France was granted territory by the same authority. Therefore politicized rituals developed to demonstrate this cosmology, which were simultaneously propaganda vehicles for strengthening national identity and belief in the right of conquest and plunder.

> Studying nature and using land effectively was a spiritual path with social virtues in a country devastated by war ... The garden theorists Jacques Boyceau de la Barauderie (1560-1633) was crucial in engineering the shift from the moral language of *mesnagement* politics to a learned language of territorial governance... Treating rational land use à la *mesnagement* traditional as an intellectual pursuit, he argued that young gardeners of talent should acquire formal education in mathematics, engineering, and classical design. Proper schooling would allow them to build French gardens with a measured orderliness that would highlight the continuities between French and classical culture and display the lawful orderliness of nature. Boyceau argued that parterres or formal gardens beds should be laid out in complex and symmetrical ways to embody the abundance and orderliness of nature as it was known to science. This design strategy was implicitly a

program of "restoration," intended to bring gardens closer to perfection using human intelligence, but Boyceau's writings presented the work as intellectual, a fruit of knowledge rather than faith. With this shift in register, he melded antiquarian and scientific forms of "rationality" with *mesnagement* techniques (Mukerji2007, 21-2).

Systems of knowledge production formed the basis of a politicized cosmology. In place of spirituality, the French developed a cosmology of land management. A cosmology that was the product of the emerging field of botany and symbol of French dominion and dominance. French gardens in France represented an idealized symbol of the Empire and promoted propaganda of the king's right to conquest as well as demonstrated his plunder.

Mesnagement, as a practice and ideology, was a demonstration of French power over nature and over Empire. French botanical gardens were demonstrative of the simultaneous control of French territory and domestication of 'exotic' specimens plundered from the colonies. In this way, "[l]and management as a legitimate principle of power took on a unique role in French politics" (Mukerji 2007, 20). In the politics of Mesnagement, the king's body became symbolic of Empire, as such "[k]eeping the king healthy was not a simple project. It tool an active search for new ingredients for his morning tonic, new cures for his constipation, and novel medicines to reduce the chronic pain he suffered in his jaw" (Mukerji 2007, 26). Mesnagement, aside from its ideological function, also served to safe guard the health of the king. In the politics and propaganda of mesnagement we see a synchronous motivation of the development of botanical gardens in France. These gardens housed 'exotic' specimens, which were essential to the development of the field of botany, medicines and the commodification of plants, which were lucrative enterprises in France (Schiebinger 13). The nation-state's project of Mesnagement and botanical gardens in France were made possible by "[c]olonial botany- the study, naming, cultivation, and marketing of plants in colonial contexts- was born of and supported European voyages, conquests, global trade, and scientific exploration" (Schiebinger and Swan 2007, 2). The form of botanical gardens represent the materialization of state intellectual policy both in enterprises within France and in its colonies as well as an ideological project that proliferated a state cosmology.

It is significant to recognize that the French nation and colonies were administered by one Imperial apparatus. In this light, it is impossible to speak of the development of a uniquely French knowledge; as knowledge production came under the centralized control that oversaw its development across and in between diverse territories that constituted the French Empire, of which France was a territory. This is counter to the common assumption of the colony as the supplier of raw materials and the metropole as the site for their development. In the botanical gardens in the imperial territory of France, plant specimens came from all over the Empire, including France and Haiti. Furthermore, their development, in terms of medicines and the economy, occurred both in France and in Haiti. As James E. McClellan (2010) argues,

> science and organized knowledge did not come to Saint Domingue as something separate from the rest of the colonizing process but, rather, formed an inherent part of French colonialism from the beginning. In other words, the French did not colonize Saint Domingue and then import science and medicine as cultural afterthoughts. French science and learning came part and parcel with French colonialism, virtually as a " productive force" (7).

In the French territory of Haiti (Saint Domingue) the mobilization of the state apparatus organized both the appropriation of plants intended for botanical gardens across the Empire as well as the appropriation of Indigenous and African knowledge that formed a hub of medical research in Haiti. University-centered

> contemporary European medicine became more firmly established in eighteenth-century Saint Domingue than anywhere else in the Americas at the time. In addition, several formal botanical gardens and experimental agricultural stations enriched the colony's scientific infrastructure ... The French military- notably the royal navy- was another colonizing

institution in Saint Domingue that made considerable use of scientific and technical knowledge, particularly in a series of astronomical and cartographic expeditions sponsored by the navy ministry, the Marine Academy at Brest, and the Royal Academy of Sciences in Paris. In these and like ways it becomes clear that science became firmly institutionalized in old Saint Domingue and a key element in government policies for colonial development (McClellan 2010, 4).

The development of French medicine and sciences was a multi-spatial initiative of the imperial state-apparatus, which through its control over knowledge production, created an ideology of French national identity and new information based industries and technologies.

The prowess of Empire to create a national identity reaches its epitome when we fail to understand how state policies and projects transcend geo-political formations and borders. The rationale of the state has never been to hurt Others for the sake and prosperity of its own citizens, and when this has occurred it has been secondary to main objectives. The imperial state seeks to hold power and territory. It is for this reason that Laurelyn Whitt (2009) argue the "pursuit of knowledge of the natural world has long been politicized" and why science has played a vital role in statecraft (xiii). In our collective awareness we have a specific imaginary of what colonialism is. It is white people killing people of colour and plundering. The pervasiveness of this imaginary is evidenced by the tendency of "historians, post-colonialist, even historians of science rarely recogniz[ing] the importance of plants to the processes that form and reform human societies and politics on a global scale" (Schiebinger quoted in Whitt 2009, 19). The ways in which scholars conduct their research about colonialism, the rationale for that research, creates a situation where the collection and study of plants by the imperial state become nearly invisible. A troubling reality given the situation where

> Not only did European naturalists collect 'the stuff of nature,' Schiebinger notes, but they also "lay their own peculiar grid of

reason over nature so that nomenclatures and taxonomies often served as 'tools of empire.'" Botanists, for their part, were 'agents of empire'; their inventories, classifications, and transplantations were the vanguard and in some cases the 'instruments' of European order.

At the same time, formal scientific institutions (such as Britain's Kew Gardens) played a crucial role in the expansion of empire by generating and disseminating scientific knowledge "which facilitated transfers of energy, manpower, and capital on a worldwide basis and on an unprecedented scale" (Whitt 2009, 19).

The imperial state-apparatus, in its focus on collecting plants and knowledge about plants formed part of a worldwide network connecting Empires in this pursuit to simultaneously colonize and establish an Imperial order. It is this simultaneity that is missed in most historical narratives. History tends to either focus on colonialism or on European history as if these are completely distinct narratives.

In dominant historiography what is missed is phenomena such as extractive biocolonialism, which "may be understood as any activity that through the use of force or coercion (economic or otherwise), involves or facilitates the removal, processing, conversion into private property, and commodification of indigenous genetic resources by agents of the dominant culture(s)" (Whitt 2009, 23). This is a practice of the imperial state. For Indigenous peoples extractive biocolonialism tends to result in

1. substantial damage to the environment, such that a peoples' way of life is destroyed, undermined, or threatened;
2. erosion of indigenous health and well-being, whether physical or spiritual;
3. destabilization of indigenous social, economic, and legal structures;
4. creation of new, or the exacerbation of existing, internal or external political struggles;
5. imposition of concepts, practices, and values that further the economic and political interests of the dominant culture
(Whitt 2009, 23).

Empire is able to disrupt peoples' relation to nature by damaging the environment and replacing Indigenous science with procedures for knowledge production, which are incompatible with the nuanced and precise science that Indigenous people have developed over many centuries. This practice erodes Indigenous social infrastructure which allows for ease in asserting authority over traditional territories. The extent extractive biocolonialism can be grasped when on considers that

> [b]y the end of the eighteenth century, Europe possessed some sixteen hundred botanical gardens connecting scientific enterprises, plant acclimatization, plant transfers, and experimentation around the world. Bourguet calls naturalists "gardeners of the earth" as they reshaped global flora by moving plants across seas and climates. The skills of botanists and horticulturalists were crucial to establishing victualing gardens along trade routes to restock trading company and naval vessels with familiar European fare. In turn, botanical gardens served as the laboratories of colonial botany. Botanists transferred plants from garden to garden around the world, building inventories and stocks of natural goods and thus facilitating the study, cultivation, and experimentation with profitable plants from all parts of the globe (Schiebinger and Swan 2007, 13).

Botanical garden were laboratories for state facilitated knowledge production for the purpose of developing information based industry and technologies. It is due to this network of international botanical gardens that corn, Indigenous to Mexico, and potatoes, Indigenous to Peru, were extracted by the Spanish empire and managed by the British Empire to control and mediate famine in Britain (Burchardt 2000 and Bisman 2012).

The management of famine as a technology of Empire

The fall of the Roman Empire left a power vacuum, which led to many wars and a long struggle between emerging nation-states. This situation coupled with the banishment of all knowledge (philosophy and science) that was not Christian doctrine, led to a devastating situation for peoples in Europe. Famine became commonplace. To mediate famine in Britain, which was a lasting legacy of the Dark ages, the British state introduced the expropriated potatoes- plundered by the Spanish Empire from the Inca nation- as an "attractive substitute for the inferior grains more common in the diets of the poor in the west" (Burchardt 2000, 673). The imperial state initiated a policy of potato grounds to supplement plot allotments, which were allotments of lands granted on a yearly basis as a means to meet social and moral obligations (Burchardt 2000, 671). Potato grounds, as a state policy, were a technology of applying the knowledge produced at botanical gardens for the practical purposes of supporting the agricultural industry. Potatoes allowed for the farmers to naturally weed their lands; and since they absorbed different nutrients from the soil than most yearly crops (such as corn), potatoes allotments allowed the soil to replenish itself.

> Furthermore, because potato grounds were let only for a season rather than, as was the case with allotments, for the whole year, they no more interfered with the following year's cultivation than did a crop of turnips. As soon as the potatoes had been lifted, the farmer would be able to plow the land and sow a corn crop as usual for the next season. Bearing in mind that historians credit these characteristics of turnips with significantly increasingly crop yields in England during the eighteenth and early nineteenth centuries, potato grounds on fallows probably not only maintained the farmer's arable output but boosted it considerably (Burchardt 2000, 675).

The technology of potato grounds allowed farmers to increase the quality and yield of their own crops, as well as collecting market rent for the use of their lands. In addition to this, the "growth of potatoes, as observed by a farmer on the chalky district, affords a means of keeping the labourers more under subjection, and prevents their leaving their master at least during the summer, as in that case the crop would be forfeited" (Eric L. Jones quoted in Burchardt 2000, 674).

The potatoes appropriated from the Inca, alongside the knowledge appropriated of this plant, formed part of a greater project of British colonialism both within the geo-political space of Britain and within the colonies of Spain. Potatoes, after being colonized (domesticated) as part of the world-wide system of botanical gardens, became part of a technology employed in Britain to bolster the agricultural industry to ameliorate agricultural yields by creating better growing conditions while indenturing poor people. Potatoes were one of many crops that the imperial state used as a means of social control within the geo-political space of Europe.

> Fogel instead suggested that most famines in England between 1500 and 1800 were 'manmade', a consequence of highly inelastic demand for food. Along similar lines, Persson used empirical data to illustrate that inventories of grain were small and transport and storage costs high, such that market failure, rather than merely harvest failure, was the primary cause of famine in pre-industrial Europe, preventing 'the desired inter-temporal and inter-spatial redistribution of grain' (Bisman 2012, 112).

The success of the botanical gardens meant that the wealth of plants and knowledge systems were available to the imperial state to use in projects across their own territories. In this respect Empires shared information, as botanical gardens formed a worldwide system, where Spanish colonialism facilitated British acquisition of the potato as a technology. However, this technology was not shared with the people of any territories. They were technologies solely developed to support market based industry. After the advent of botanical gardens, and the dissemination of their research, famine itself became a technology of the state. These technologies were manufactured by extractive colonialism of the Americas and implemented in the space of Europe. Famine, as a Imperial project, emerged as a technology by way of botanical gardens of colonialism. In particular, the imperial state-apparatus introduced the potato- plant and cultivating knowledge appropriated from the Inca- as intellectual property shared between the Spanish and British Empires- to facilitate population control and genocide of the Irish, while bolstering the agricultural industry and maintaining a cosmology that normalized colonialism and kingdoms through the practice of mesnagement.

As European nation-states consolidated, a renewed urgency in conquest began, thus ushering the age of European colonialism of the Americas. Colonialism, as defined by OED is the "policy or practice of acquiring full or partial political control over another country, occupying it with settlers, and exploiting it economically"[iii]. This definition gives the impression that colonialism, its mechanisms and rationale, occurred exclusively outside of the geo-political space of Europe. Colonialism is defined as an occurrence that involves Europeans colonizing Other spaces. This idea leads to a perception that the space of colonialism is never within the geo-political space of European nation-states. A perspective that eludes the ways in which European nation-states were simultaneously Imperial colonizing states, who first colonized Europe, who broke apart Indigenous and traditional communal forms to assert itself and attain power. Policies developed by European nation-states were simultaneously Imperial policies applied both within and outside of the geo-political space of Europe.

PART FIVE:
Perceiving convergence

The disavowal of colonialism asks us to consider how to encounter stories- that is narratives based on what the historian values and his intentions in writing- that are produced by the academic discipline of history? I say stories quite intentionally. My intention is to highlight the belief that historical narratives have a direct relation to what has happened in the past, which is a belief in scientific historiography. This is the belief that historical narratives are strictly about the past and produced by the objective historian. A belief that is the tenet of the realist historiography. Realism is based on the belief in the necessity of a scientific historiography. To call research scientific, or to say that a scientific method was employed, is to create the idea that research was done with excellence, rigour, and in strict adherence to a scientific standard. A goal of the realist paradigm is to establish history as a science because it invalidates the idea of history as a story, as having anything to do with the discipline of literature. To be connected to the discipline of literature suggests that there might be an element of creativity in the process of historical research, which is intolerable to most historians. In the realist paradigm history can never be a story. However, as we have seen in dominant historical narratives of the university, there is no shared methodology, no common adherence to a scientific standard. Therefore, the narratives produced are distinct, not what one would expect of a science. If not a science, then what is the practice of history?

To say that there is an absolute difference between the disciplines of history and literature is based on the idea that history is based in reality and literature is a fiction. This difference is more imaginary than descriptive when one evaluates the end product of each. For Roland Barthes (1981), when we look at the writing produced by these disciplines there is little distinction to be found. For Barthes (1981), the discourses of history and literature are indistinguishable. Barthes (1981) suggests that we must

> [g]ive an answer to the question whether structural analysis is justified in retaining the traditional typology of discourses; whether it is fully legitimate to make a constant opposition

between the discourses of poetry and the novel, the fictional narrative and the historical narrative (7).

Immediately you might think, yes there is a justification in making a strict distinction between the fictional and historical narrative. Yes, there must be a strict distinction between the novel and the history textbook, and the distinction must rest on how the historian writes about what has happened based on historical facts- suspending at least slightly how messy historical facts are. At this juncture, it seems significant to consider the relative similarity between the historical narrative and historical novel, both use what we can all agree are historical events or occurrences. To this I would ask you, how you know that historical facts represent actual events (were you there to bear witness)? And conversely, why do you assume that the novel does not attest to events that have taken place over the whole expanse of human history (are you able to say with absolute certainty that the occurrences narrated in novels are completely made up)? At the very least one must consider that the historical novel, in particular, points to the relative indistinction between the disciplines of history and literature.

Moreover, if we look at the very different narratives of the history of the university, we can see that these are stories structured by the values and intentions of the historian. In this way, these narratives are produced by way of the subjective values and intentions of the historian. Historical narratives are given their identity in the subjective work of the historian. Much like what gives the identity to literature is the author. As Barthes(1981) argues

> [a]s we can see, simply from looking at its structure and without having to invoke the substance of its content, historical discourse is in its essence a form of ideological elaboration, or to put it more precisely, an *imaginary* elaboration ... We can appreciate as a result why it is that the notion of a historical 'fact' has often aroused a certain degree of suspicion in various quarters. Nietzche said in his time: 'There are no facts in themselves. It is always necessary to begin by introducing a meaning in order that there can be a fact.' From the moment that language in involved (and when is it not involved?), the fact can only be defined in a tautological fashion: what is noted

> derives from the notable, but the notable is only- from Herodotus onwards, when the word lost its accepted mythic meaning- what is worthy of recollection, that is to say, worthy of being noted (16-7).

For Barthes (1981) the fact cannot be a legitimate distinguishing feature to segregate the novel from the historical text. The fact is only ever exemplary of the cultural paradigm of the author; the fact exists because someone has taken note of it because it was deemed noteworthy.

Moreover, what unites writing in general is its imaginary quality in so far as all writing stems from the author, his values and intention, his ordering of events, the tone and style of his writing. When we encounter writing, we are encountering the author; the story is derivative of the relation between the author and their writing. Therefore it is incumbent on us to let go of the ideal of a truth test. In other words, it is of little relevance to (e)valuate historical narratives based on whether they are truthful or not. It is simply an impossible task. It is however relevant to understand why and how authors write. This is particularly true in the situation where different authors who take different historiographical approaches to write vastly distinct narratives about the same topic. It is exceptionally necessary when authors who write vastly different narratives all manage to uphold the same core belief. Realist historians of the university we have encountered take different approaches- abstract and tangible contexts. Yet despite these significant variations, all these historians maintain a singular commonality: they all believe that the university is uniquely European, suggesting a serious problem in the desire for an objective historiography promoted by the realist paradigm.

The subjective quality of history has long since been a central issue that critical historiography engages. The idea of the subjective historian is paramount. Some, like Ranke, believe that the subjective historian is a betrayal of objective history. Others believe that the entire process of history is subjective, from the creation of the archives (Trouillot), data analysis (Bradley1968) to writing

(Barthes 1981). The issue of the subjectivity of the historian is also a discussion of philosophy. Realism advances the idea that it is not only possible, but desirable, to rid history of any elements of the philosophical by employing a scientific methodology. Realism suggests that it is possible to consolidate facts about the past, and that these facts would form the canon of the discipline of history.

However, to this position, scholars, such as Fulda (2010), argue that history is the practice of philosophy, as history emerges from a cultural worldview, a metaphysics, which becomes how people interact with reality. Often, the philosophical elements- worldview, paradigm, metaphysics- that substantiate the discipline of history are based on colonialism. The philosophical elements of dominant history are founded on the logic of separation and dualistic thinking (hooks). Alternative narratives also tend to function within similar dualistic reasoning. If normative histories deny colonialism, then alternative histories focus on colonialism. If histories are based on colonial archives, then the task of the new historian is to amass a different archive. If histories are written from the viewpoint of the European colonizer, then an alternative history should be written from the Other's viewpoint. If history is written from the rationale of the ruling class, then history should expose its social infrastructure. While these historians write alternative narratives they do not challenge the presuppositions of the discipline of history. In particular, within these approaches what persists is the core belief in an objective historian.

This position necessarily ignores the temporal disjuncture in the historian's work. The historian is in the present as he creates a narrative about the past. His narrative is a careful construction based on a particular sequencing of what he validates as facts about the past. Since, as Bradley (1968) argues, facts are theories, their validation is not a given; validation is rather a process the historian undertakes in the present about the past. It is the process that centers the historian's subjective truth tests. For Bradley (1968), "everything that we say we think we have reasons, our realities are built up of explicit or hidden inferences; in a single word, our facts are inferential, and their actuality depends on the correctness of the reasoning which makes then what they are" (90). This is not a scientific process that follows the principles of a scientific method. Generally in the sciences, the scientist formulates a thesis, and through experiment validates or discredits his thesis. The fundamental premise of this method is that any other scientist, following the same experiments will achieve the same results. In other words, the scientific method presupposes that conclusions are verifiable and experiments can be duplicated. As such, the scientific method has built into it the idea of validity testing. No such process exists in the field of history. The historian evaluates the facts based on his own criteria and arrives at a judgment that is utterly unique to his own thought process, and the paradigm that has informed this process.

If not an explicit process, how is it that the historian judges the validity of facts? Bradley (1968) argues that he does so by the same means that he judges everything else, by his own personal, and often implicit, reasoning process. For Bradley (1968), the " common experience of reasonable beings bears us out in the assertion that we do not believe without a reason; that the fact asserted by another remains in its position, as an asserted fact, unless we have some cause to take it as true, and to make it a part of our own world" (94). The historian judges the validity of historical facts based on his own process of reasoning, which is an accumulation of experiences. He uses the substance of his own life, his personal experience and accumulated knowledge base, to validate facts. The actual process of the historian reveals that in practice the temporal disjuncture is not of the past but in the present. The practice of the historian is rather a complex dialogue from which the historian acts a temporal interloper. For Bradley (1968), "'[t]he historian', it may be objected, 'does perhaps as critical divide the world of the past (as in the proper sense not yet known) from the present and known world; but the process is illusory" (101-2). Any perceived division between the past- the object of the historian's analysis and judgment- and the present- the context of his being and work- is an illusion. The historian straddles both temporalities; he is a time traveler, of sorts. The meaning he derives from the object of his analysis is only meaningful in the present. In other words, the historian's process is the creation of analogies as "history is incapable of attesting to events without analogy in the present world" (Bradley 1968, 103). The historian derives meaning to the extent that he can make past occurrences resonate by way of analogy with his own life.

In essence, the work of the historian is critical observation of past occurrence. It is not the passive collection and ordering of historical data. Disciplined learning- based on the logic of separation- dictates that learning adhere to disciplinary borders. Without the appearance of objective research and analysis, there is very little or anything at all that separates history from the field of literature. If the historian subjectively uses his own life as the criteria for evaluating historical facts, then the narrative is not easily labeled as objective history. This is a crucial border that is fading. It is a border that is threatened by the subjectivity of the historian, as it calls into questions the difference between fiction and history. Maintaining these strict disciplinary borders is often derived from an impulsive need to protect the structure of the university. It is a desire to endow practices with a scientific sub-context thereby dispelling any connection between the discipline of history to the field of literature or philosophy. This is however, a near impossible endeavour.

> We have seen the reason why every history is necessarily based upon prejudication; and experiences testifies that, as a matter of fact, there is no single history which is not so based, which does not derive its individual character from the particular standpoint of the author. There is no such thing as a history without a prejudication; the real distinction is between the writer who has his prejudication without knowing what they are, and whose prejudications, it may be, are false, and the writer who consciously orders and creates from the known foundation of that which for him is the truth (Bradley 1968, 96).

For Bradley (1968) there is no doubt that history is written from the standpoint of the author. He is not concerned with maintaining the disciplinary border between history and literature. His focus is to make a critical distinction between the historian who consciously engages the present in the process of his work and the other who is content to believe that his work is solely about the past. For Bradley (1968), the critical historian is conscious of their status as temporal interloper. This type of historicism is based on understanding that the

> ultimate real object, the final reference and last basis, is constituted by that which has been, or can be, personally verified in our own external or internal critical observation. If we are asked for the reason of our beliefs we are sooner or later in the last resort brought back to this; and it is thus our immediate personal (though that need not mean our individual) experience, on which, by many steps or by few, all our certainty depends (Bradley 1968, 103).

A key presupposition of a critical historiography, for Bradley (1968), is the critical mind of the temporal interloper, the historian who transcends the social constructions of linear time; the historian who actively engages her experiences as historical method.

We are then brought to the question of what constitutes personal experience. Bradley (1968) makes a crucial distinction between personal and individual experiences. Individual experiences, for our purposes, are experiences that belong to the person, that is, experiences that occur in their own lifetime and impact them directly. In contrast, personal experiences are our individual experiences contextualized in the structures of their formation. For Bradley (1968), personal experiences are

> [t]he contents which in early life are taken into and build up our consciousness, consisting as they do of our individual experiences blended into one substance inextricably with the experiences of others, exist in the uncritical mind as that which (for itself at least) is a confused and unsystematized world of consciousness. It is to such a world that the critical intelligence awakens, and its awakening is the sundering of its material from itself (102).

Personal experience is thus experienced reality; it is the totality of that which we have lived, including how these experiences interact with the experiences of others. These experiences may for some be recalled to form a state of confusion and chaos; however, to the critical mind personal experience is a wealth of knowledge that the critical historian seeks to unpack and express.

In essence we are dealing with the totality of a person's memories and concrete occurrences of individual experience. "In psychological terms, memory describes the processes that are used by the brain for the long-term storage of information. Early studies implicated both transcription and translation as important for the formation of long-term memories" (Levenson and Sweatt 2005, 113). In other words, memories have a biological context. At the cellular level, memories are recorded (through transcription) and recalled (through translation). This is a process, which until recently, was believed to occur in real time, meaning, that lived experiences are transcribed onto cells in 'real' time, where they are stored for translation, memory recollection. However, "relevant data from the few extant neurobiology-related studies have already indicated a theme- epigenetic mechanisms probably have an important role in synaptic plasticity and memory formation" (Levenson and Sweatt 2005, 108). The old model of cell division and differentiation was that a cell, containing DNA- the genetic code of a person- went through processes of cell division and differentiation while a person was maturing. As we grow cells divide to create new cells which become differentiated into liver cells, brain cells, lung cells and so forth. Each cell replicates DNA according to its epigenetic markers. Epigenetics is in essence cell memory, how a cell remembers how to become a liver cell, brain cell, lung cell and so forth. DNA is believed to be constant, the biological coding we inherit from our parents, while epigenetic markers were believed to be mutable given the reality of our life-situation (108). The old realist model suggested that epigenetic markers were 'erased' during conception, and babies received a 'clean slate' (Thomson 2015). The old realist model suggested that epigenetic markers were no longer in use during processes of cell division and differentiation after full maturation. In the old realist model, once we reach adulthood, epigenetic markers changed function and then exclusively coded our cells with behavioural memory.

Recent research in the field of epigenetics has shown that the old model is mistaken. Babies are not born with a clean slate. Babies are born with a specific epigenetic inheritance (Thomson 2015). Researchers have found that epigenetic markers that code behavioural memory in adults are passed onto children. Once such study has shown that "genetic changes stemming from the trauma suffered by Holocaust survivors are capable of being passed on to their children, the clearest sign yet that one person's life experience can affect subsequent generations" (Thomson 2015). In humans "the transmission of trauma to a child via what is called 'epigenetic inheritance'" (Thomson 2015). Children's epigenetic inheritance furnishes children with an increased number of receptors, meaning that children of parents who endured trauma are more sensitive to trauma; their cells are coded to more readily identify and react to trauma.

This research in the field of epigenetics suggests that personal memory is intergenerational memory, and inherently historical. Suggesting that history is always already within us. For the critical historian the field of epigenetics appears to justify the process of drawing on personal experience as part of addressing the inherent disjuncture of time in history. This represents alternative epistemological paradigm that runs counter to the logic of separation. It is the insertion of a paradigm of convergence in the practice of history; since there is no procedural disconnect between the historian and history. The critical historian who looks within instinctively knows that her connection surpasses her own lived experiences. For Bradley (1968), "[c]ritical history assumes that its world is one, and that in that world exists, and has but to demonstrate the existence of itself" (97). In this way, critical research is not creative, in the sense that it creates the past. It is rather expository in so far as it documents the connection of a world where experiences are interconnected and never separable. This exposition is legitimate in so far as our experiences are understood to be part of the living whole; a wholeness whose context includes spatial and temporal unity. The ability to see the whole is a presupposition of critical historiography; manifested in the unwillingness of the critical historian to delegitimize the logic of separation while valuing their personal experiences and perception of the totality of history.

Converging historical narratives is a move away from dominant historical narratives based in realism. For most historians, the archives substantiate research and legitimize the practice of history. The archives form the cornerstone of the research process. It is a process that is premised on the idea that history emerges from archives. In this process the historian is an objective facilitator. It is not he who is creating history, but rather he is the one telling the story of the archives. In this paradigm, it is the historian who writes the narrative contained within the archives. The process of creating converging histories expands the research scope of the historian. Instead of a neat archive, a historiography that may facilitate the converging of narratives centers the subjective interpretation of the historian. There is no defined scope of research- such as the archive; no particular space to focus on- such as a country, no temporal frame- such as a decade. A historiography of converging histories is dependent on the subjective analysis of the historian, a proposition that may be seen as counter to what responsible history should be.

Perception is crucial for the critical historian. To perceive takes on an extra-sensory function. It involves being aware of one's own life in terms of the totality of one's experiences as well as contextualizing those experiences; "[w]e see what we perceive and the object of our perceptions is qualified by the premises of our knowledge, by our previous experiences" (Bradley 1968, 91).

Perception becomes a function of a complex ability to be aware. To perceive becomes an extension of our cognition of personal, intergeneration, experiences. We perceive and interpret reality based on our lives- grounded by the accumulation of intergenerational experiences coded epigenetically. Perception is much more than seeing an object or an externality. To perceive is to be aware of reality within the context of intergenerational experiences and our psychological, biological predisposition to perceive according to our ancestral inheritance. It is in our ability to fully know ourselves that we equip ourselves to approach history critically. As we perceive history through our intergenerational experience we bring a unique perspective to the discipline of history and challenge its disciplinary tactics formed from within the realist paradigm.

Perceiving Colonialism

Empire includes a bureaucracy that administers the conversion of stolen wealth and knowledge from the colonies into Imperial resources and technologies. It oversees the conversion of Imperial robbery genocide into capital. One way Imperial states do this is by creating the conditions of possibility for the emergence of intellectual life by supporting the university's development with capital in the form of wealth and appropriated knowledge. Universities are colonial sites where capital wealth develops the infrastructure of the university and plundered knowledge is converted into intellectual property. Simultaneously the university facilitates dominant narratives that disavow this relationship between the university and colonialism.

The change from appropriated knowledge into intellectual property has occurred as the conversion of Alexander's conquest and plunder of the Persian Empire into the foundation of the European intellectual tradition; appropriated Islamic wealth, philosophy and science, by Christian crusaders, enabling the Renaissance; appropriated Arabic philosophy and science- from cities such as Al-Andalus- for dissemination throughout Europe supporting the development of the oldest universities in Europe (Oxford, Paris, Bologna); and biocolonialism of Indigenous Sovereignties into the fields of botany, medicine and technology development. These moments in the development of the university are exemplary of colonialism as the condition of possibility for intellectual innovation in European universities.

This has been my perception of colonialism, my awareness of history. I have written based on the belief that history is always already within us. It is not the history that one might find in textbooks. When we begin within, we bring a unique perspective to the practice of history. When we begin within and go beyond, we cannot help but create conscious and critical history. Critical history is premised on the practice of the historian's inference as historical awareness. For Bradley (1968), a presupposition of critical history is that the historian's inference occurs in the present; the work of evaluating evidence happens in the present, as does the historian's reasoning that leads her to a specific conclusion. This reasoning is not akin to any scientific process; but rather, based on her personal experience. The critical historian perceives reality based on her personal experience. Where her personal experience is an integration of intergenerational experiential knowledge encoded in her genes by way of epigenetic cellular mechanisms (Matthen 2005, 2013). Her perception is her "sensory systems [as] automatic sorting machines that come into direct contact with environmental objects and sort them into classes according to how they should be treated for the purposes of physical manipulation and investigation" (Matthen 2005, 10). Our perception of reality, how we manipulate and investigate reality, occurs within, across space and time. Our perception of personal experiences is inherently of the body-occurring through the interface of our sensory receptors as our cells encode our memories that are added to the memories of our ancestors.

For the critical historian, history is a living entity. It is however, not alive; history is a haunting. It is a haunting where presence is always felt, perceived, but not manifest. It is for the conscious spirit a yearning for meaning, to express what lingers in the ether. It is the silent clamour of the witches, whores and pagans whose pyres lay the foundation of Europe. As Derrida (1993) writes

> [t]he ghostly would displace itself like the movement of this history Haunting would mark the very existence of Europe. It would open the space of what is called by this name, at least since the Middle Ages. The experience of the specter, that is how Marx, along with Engels, will have also thought, described, or diagnosed a certain dramaturgy of modern Europe, notably that of its great unifying projects. One would even have to say that he represented it or staged it (3).

The beauty in Marx was his ability to chart history as a haunting. Marx was concerned with the plague of alienation, his historical analysis named its source, the development of the capitalist mode of production as the great unifying project of modern Europe. This was Marx's unique perspective, fueled by his personal experience of poverty, which he socialized in *Capital*. The brilliance of Marx was his ability to sense the haunting of previous social and economic cultures that burned to fertilize the ground for capitalism- although his work did not fully enunciate this. Marx could sense that the economic and social cultures of capitalism were destructive; he was aware what others theorized as normal relations of production and exchange were unreasonable.

> To sense is truly a magical gift. Our senses are biological systems that evolved to give organisms an advantage by providing them with the means by which to respond effectively to the challenges of living and reproducing in surroundings that are constantly in flux. Thought of in this way, the senses are not simply information-sinks- organs that happen to receive ambient information at their sensory receptors, leaving their possessors to determine how to use this information. Nor are they engineered to seek information optimal for the organism's pre-existing needs. Rather, they are evolved systems (Matthen 2015, 24).

Our senses are intergenerational ways of knowing, which predispose us to meet the challenges and adapt based on our ancestral cumulative knowing. Marx's ability to sense allowed him to uniquely understand the social and economic realty of capitalism. He acutely sensed the history of its development and its manifestation; he saw clearly the specter of capital, the haunting of cultures and peoples who were sacrificed at the altar of capital. Marx is a critical historian; although his perspective was, in *Capital*, limited to the ideological space of Europe.

However, this was not the trajectory of his intellectual development. In the last years of his life, Marx was not content to criticize capitalism in Europe. His attention turned to understanding communal economies as alternatives to the capitalist mode of production, in particular, the social and economic structure of the Haudenosaunee peoples (Rosemount). His attention turned away from criticism to imagining possibilities for a solution in Europe by learning from Others- notwithstanding that this attempt was deeply clouded by a Eurocentric bias and racism. Marx could perceive the possibility of another way forward.

> Perception for us is action of two kinds. First, it is for guidance of the body as it interacts with other material objects. Second, it is for finding out about things in the world, for building up a record of the characteristics of such objects, and forming expectations concerning how they will behave in the future. The main thesis to be advanced builds the content of perception on what it tells us about how objects should be treatedwith respect to these goals. To put it very briefly, the thesis is that sensory systems are automatic sorting machines that come into direct contact with environmental objects and sort them into classes according to how they should be treated for the purposes of physical manipulation and investigation (Matthen 2005, 14).

Perception is then a conscious awareness of external occurrences and states of affairs as well as a predictive ability on how to manipulate or investigate that which is perceived. Marx perceived another reality, another way of being. However, his perception was of course based on his personal experiences, which were clouded and therefore, Marx could not escape the logic of his culture, the logic of hierarchy and separation. Nonetheless, his focus late in life can be seen as an invitation, his plea for future scholars to find a solution to the problem of capitalism. Perhaps those of us drawn to this plea are those who Derrida (1993) anticipates.

> Anticipating the coming, one day, one night, several centuries later, of another "scholar." The latter would finally be capable, beyond the opposition between presence and non-presence, actuality and inactuality, life and non-life, of thinking the possibility of the specter, the specter as possibility. Better (or worse) he would know how to address himself to spirits (13).

Perhaps we are collectively anticipating (an)Other scholar whose conscious perception includes an awareness of the haunting of conquest as it presents itself in our own lives. It is our hope that (an)Other scholar, a critical historian, might perceive, may intuitively be aware of the totality of experienced reality. That she may go within to discover the world around her.

For most of us, to go within is to acknowledge trauma, to recognize that our irrational fears are completely rational; it is a gift. It is a gift from our ancestors that we may acutely perceive the haunting and continuity of colonialism. Within our own bodies is embedded intergenerational knowledge and ways of knowing. It is the task of the critical historian to move past the cultural logics of separation, to perceive the wholeness of the world; to sense the haunting of our ancestors; to pay attention to what we feel and recognize the inherent wealth always already within us.

Conceptualizing colonialism

I am writing my perception of colonialism. It is my thinking about colonialism; it is how I contextualize my personal experiences of colonialism. I have chosen to discuss colonialism as a concept. What follows is an unstructured conceptual analysis of colonialism based on a large scale of space and time. I do not make particular arguments. I make general propositions for your consideration. Not a consideration of whether it is true or not, but rather a consideration of its relevance to your own thoughts and to a broader discussion of colonialism. I am not writing a definitive theory of colonialism. I am also not writing a subjective and individual account of colonialism. I am not writing in that way because it would likely create closures, and suggest that our experiences are divergent. I am writing for you to consider our experiences as similar, and also to consider how that similarity attests to the specificity of colonial policies and technologies. This type of consideration is open to the possibility of a convergent analysis of colonialism.

Colonialism is a system that creates conditions for its continuity. This continuity is produced through ideological iterations that fix narratives of colonization as divergent. Colonialism is a set of logics, policies and technologies intent on subjugating nations. A subjugated nation is a nation of colonized peoples. It is a situation where people themselves become the mechanisms, or conditions of possibility, for the continuity of colonial relations. Sustaining divergent narratives, experiences and knowledge about colonization is a tactic to isolate resistance and is an ideal situation for the continuity of colonial relations.

Colonialism is about consuming life; which necessitates the destruction of matrilineal and matriarchal cultures that are premised on a deep respect and love of the sacred balance of life. Colonialism is about establishing one way of life that consumes the earth; which necessitates eradicating traditional cultures that live harmoniously with the land. Colonialism thrives on instilling a deep sense of terror in people and offering sanctuary from that terror: citizenship and belonging to the state. Colonialism has only been a successful project in Europe. The very idea of Europe is premised on the erasure of history while constructing Europe as a distinct geography and people. This is a disavowal of the ways in which Europe is founded on and made possible by the appropriation of knowledge by way of colonialism, conquest and plunder. Moreover, European consciousness has developed not only based on these erasures, but suffers because of them. They do not know who they are- the descendants of traditional peoples with knowledge of the land, medicines and the stars. This history and knowledge has been stripped from their awareness.

To be colonized is to become the colonizer. It is not only to ignore one's relation to the land, but to turn against her; to actively participate in her destruction. It is to offer no thanks for her blessings, to take beyond your need, to celebrate over consumption. To become a colonizer is a deeply personal process. For some it is instantaneous, it occurs at the moment of terror, it is trauma encoded so deeply that it becomes who you are. For others, it takes generations of encoded trauma to create a sufficient level of terror to create the pathology of the colonizer. Once terror is there, it festers, it is an infection that reaches your heart, and once there, you no longer tremble from fear, but take pleasure in your absolute abandonment of yourself as you become the site of terror, the cause of trauma. To be colonized is to actively remove oneself from cycles of life, nutrition, and love. It is to fester in the abyss of colonial imaginaries, to slowly decay in place where time has no meaning. To be colonized, however, is not a permanent state of being.

Europe is a colonial success. It is the only one on Earth. Europe is a colonial success because people believe themselves to be European. In doing so they actively forget that their ancestors suffered colonialism. Europeans forget that they have ancestors. They forget the history of being torn from the land. Of having their social structures invaded, invalidated. Their cosmologies demonized. They create distance from the history of burning millions of wise women, healers, and midwives, their ancestral matriarchy. They celebrate the version of history that tells them about the triumph of progress in the defeat of paganism and ignorance. They ignore those moments in history where the death and torture of their ancestors were the conditions of possibility for the emergence of institutions, of universities, of medicine. They celebrate being European. They support their states in their ongoing projects of colonization. They eagerly defend the need for social cleansing; they attack the social structures of free Roma and Sami nations, for instance; they cannot tolerate their proximity, it causes of quiet discomfort that masquerades as cultural intolerance. They do not recognize that what they are feeling is hatred for themselves. They do not want to see, hear, smell, feel and remember anything that might suggest that Europe has not always been, that something else existed before Europe that was full of strength, wisdom and resilience. And so they are Europeans, they have become the colonizers and with their migrations, began new colonial iterations.

Space of Colonialism

Colonial iterations are new trajectories of the same logics, policies, and technologies. The space of coloniality is the space of inception and continuity. The space of colonialism is always the space of iteration. It is the space in which colonialism infuses social relations with meaning and trajectory. It is a site for transformation, of encoding human interaction with ideologies and processes of colonialism. For Bhabha (2004) this site is the *signifying lag*. It is the space of signification that simultaneously erases the Other and creates the colonizing self. It is a signifying process that ideologically creates the conditions of possibility for the continuity of colonial relations. To signify human relations in the *signifying lag* is to superimpose ideas of superiority/inferiority, of self/other. It is to create colonial relationality as a priori to the inception of relations, ensuring that all forms of relationality are encoded with the logic and paradigm of colonialism. Jodi A Byrd (2011) theorizes this space of iteration as the *transit of Indianess*. Byrd's (2011) *Transit of Empire: Indigenous Critiques of Colonialism* develops an analysis of the state of human beings under conditions of settler colonialism. Byrd (2011) argues that settler colonialism is contingent on *Indianess as transit*. *Indianess* becomes the ideological context for the emergence of representations for settlers, diasporicarrivants, and Indigenous peoples. "As a transit, Indianess becomes a site through which U.S. empire orients and replicates itself by transforming continual reiterations of pioneer logics" (Byrd 2011). *Indianess*, for Byrd, is a static site that induces the (re)-production of pioneer logics. Moreover, Byrd (2011) argues that

> [i]n the wake of this transit, and indeed as its quality as colonialist practice, one finds discordant and competing representations of diasporic arrivals and native lived experiences- what I call cacophony- that vie for hegemony within the discursive, cultural, and political processes of representation (xiii).

Indianess becomes the site from which discordant narratives emerge and acquire their trajectories (Byrd 2011). For Byrd (2011), *Indianess as transit* is the site that formulates and echoes ideologies of the *Indian*, ideologies that form the foundations of all colonial subjectivities. While each subjectivity has its own narrative, their content and trajectory emerge from the *transit of Indianess*. These divergent colonial subjectivities create a social cacophony as they are incoherent to one another. However, as an amalgamation, these divergent narratives work to sustain the settler logics that legitimize colonial relations (Byrd 2011).

In Byrd's (2011) *Indianess as transit* and Bhabha's (2004) *signifying lag* we have convergent conceptualizations of the spatiality of colonialism. The conceptualizations are convergent in that they both describe a similar idea that colonial relations acquire their meaning and trajectory from a space that transcends the material and ideological. It is a signifying process that encodes colonial relations as social relations. Byrd's (2011) *Indianess as transit* and Bhabha's (2004) *signifying lag* conceptualize the space of colonialism as both creative and prescriptive. It is prescribed, for Byrd as the amalgamation of all ideologies of what it means/has meant/will mean to be *Indian*, and for Bhabha (2004) it is the conscious erasure of the Other and colonialism. The space of colonialism is also creative, as Byrd (2011) argues for the continuity of settler colonialism and its pioneer logics, while for Bhabha (2004) it was the condition of possibility for the emergence of modernity.

Temporality of Colonialism

To study temporality is to look at the ways in which time is cut. Byrd's (2011) *Indianess as transit* and Bhabha's (2004) *signifying lag* conceptualize the temporality as recursive time that is cut off from natural time in the process of signification. Byrd's (2011) *Indianess as transit* and Bhabha's (2004) *signifying lag* are convergent is the way they conceptualize the temporality of colonialism. Both premise their conceptualization on the idea that time in colonial relations is not linear. Because colonial relations are iterative, they exceed linear development of time. The excess is the temporality of signification. The process of signification is beyond natural time, as natural time is a shared temporality. Signification occurs instead of this shared temporality as it is recursive and defies the cumulative experience. The recursive temporality in Byrd's (2011) *Indianess as transit* and Bhabha's (2004) *signifying lag* is the temporality of the signifying process that exceeds linear time.

The temporality of colonialism in Byrd's (2011) *Indianess as transit* and Bhabha's (2004) *signifying lag* is cyclical. It is repetitive. As such, the temporality of colonialism, its cycles of signification, disrupts the communal experience of time. It pulls people outside of a fundamental shared human experience, our development in relation to time. Through its iterations, such as of *Indianess* (Byrd 2011) and modernity (Bhabha 2004), the development of human societies becomes the development of colonialism. In other words, the iterations of colonial logics, policies and technologies create human social relations as colonial relations. We confront one another as different colonial subjectivities with different experiences of colonialism (Byrd 2011). The struggle for representation in the colonial context, while created by the same ideology of *Indianess*, is structured as the struggle between divergent subjective experiences (Byrd 2011). As such, the extent to which the subjective colonial iteration is prioritized time develops as a recursive. It is a colonial temporality that colonizes our shared experience into iterative time.

Convergent relationality

Byrd's (2011) solution begins with disrupting the iterations of colonialism. Byrd (2011) envisions a movement from cacophony to convergence. For Byrd (2011), the cacophony of divergent subjectivities is formed by way of signifying iterations through the *transit of Indianess.* Instead, she suggests that Indigenous decolonization can be a process for the creation of harmonious international meetings that focus on mutual recognition of grief endured as a result of U.S. Empire. For Byrd (2011), convergence begins with mutual grieving. She argues, "it is time to imagine Indigenous decolonization as a process that restores and allows settler, arrivant, and native to apprehend and grieve together the violences of U.S. empire" (Byrd 2011, 229). To disrupt the cacophonous struggle over representation, Byrd (2011) argues for a narrative of a convergent shared experience of U.S. Empire. Byrd's temporal scheme prioritizes how colonialism has disrupted time, halted time, and created confusion; while inadvertently opening spaces that allow for the temporality of decolonization to emerge as the temporality of the convergence grief.

Byrd's work is a synthesis whose project is transformation. She argues that it is precisely through moments of difference, similarity, and tension that disciplines can reach theoretical convergence by entering a conversation (Byrd 2011). For Byrd (2011), this convergence can occur by

> placing indigenous phenomenologies into conversation with critical theory in order to identify indigenous transits and consider possible alternative strategies for legibility ... One such strategy is to read cacophonies of colonialism as they are rather than to attempt to hierarchize then into coeval or causal order. Southeastern indigenous phenomenologies understand the Middle World (the reality we all inhabit) as a bridge between Upper and Lower Worlds of creation, when boundaries between worlds break down and the distinctive characteristics of each world begin to collapse upon and bleed into the others, possibilities for rejuvenation and destruction emerge to transform the world radically. The goal is to find balance. To understand the dualistic pairings of this dynamic system is to understand, as Cherokee scholar Daniel Heath Justice has argued, 'its necessary complementarity; it is a dynamic and relational perspective, not assumption of unitary supremacy (Byrd xxvii).

For Byrd to put indigenous phenomenologies and critical theory in conversation is to have a conversation about the world as it is. Her consideration of alternative strategies centers the collapse of the timelessness of iterative cycles of colonialism. Instead of colonial subjectivities as the paradigm with which we engage the world, Byrd (2011) chooses to focus on trauma, grief, and loss. She believes that this shift in focus can be the space and temporality of Indigenous decolonization, of creating a new legibility. Grief and trauma become the common space for the emergence of a relational convergence.

A relational convergence is to see oneself from within and beyond. It requires a break from the logic of separation, of hierarchy, of origins. It is simply to see things as they are. Not as we wish them to be, but as we perceive and experience them. This approach knows no exteriority. It doubts the logics, policies and technologies of colonialism that have instilled a belief that one is disconnected from the land, from community, and from oppression. It is to suspend dualistic thinking of the dominator culture (hooks). It is a refusal to see the world as marked by divergence. It is to look for another way to encounter oneself from within and beyond. In the situation of competing colonial subjectivities, it is to encounter our trauma and the colonizer in their trauma. It is also to understand that trauma is atemporal, it haunts and torments across generations. In this way we can see trauma as the common experience of people in the context of colonialism.

A relational perspective refuses the iterations of colonialism. For Byrd (2011) to break iterations of colonial logics is to seek an alternative strategy for legibility. Within the cacophony we are only legible to one another through the *transit of Indianess* (Byrd 2011). In other words, we only recognize each other by way of the pioneer logics that structure our subjectivities. That is all we know of each other. In the cacophony we do not meet in real time or space. We meet in the endless cycles of colonial iterations. The cacophony drowns out anything; any other part of ourselves, that may prove to be harmonious, or in concert. The cacophony relies on trajectories of divergent narratives. To create communal narratives of trauma in symphony is to channel energy into processing and responding to reality. A symphony of trauma can be a convergence of narratives of survival and resilience. In symphony, in healing trauma, lies the possibility of healing the ruptures of time and space necessary for colonialism.

Decolonization is ultimatelt the convergence of resistance. It is through convergent narratives of colonialism, through sharing our personal experiences that we can begin to name the logics, policies and technologies of the international infrastructure of imperial states. Through naming we find our collective language of resistance and build convergent models of resistance. We also develop a sensibility about colonization, about being colonized.

When we write we commit to page a certain version of ourselves. I write to meet the academic mind where it is for the most part; in the logic of separation and desiring a way out. I have not told you anything new; I have facilitated your awareness of what you already perceived. I have done this for you in the same I have done it for myself. I have mourned colonialism, its iterations that have structured my life. Mourning

> consists always in attempting to ontologize remains, to make them present, in the first place by *identifying* the bodily remains and by *localizing* the dead (all ontologizing, all semanticization- philosophical, hermeneutical, or psychoanalytic- finds itself caught up by this work of mourning but, as such, it does not yet think it; we are posing here the question of the specter, to the specter ... on this near side of such thinking). One has to know. *One has to know it. One has to have knowledge* [Il faut savoir]. Now, to know is to know *who* and *where*, to know whose body it really is and what place it occupies- for it must stay in its place. In a safe place (Derrida 1993, 9).

To mourn is to give presence of the haunting of colonialism. To embody or make real that which exists neither dead or alive; the souls cry for their trauma to be known; for their families to know, to perceive the brutality of their lives. The dead bodies accumulating during the procession of colonialism demand to be known; they insist on having an impact in the present moment; they will not rest until we, their grandchildren have learned their lessons and are well armed to end the procession of death, terror and trauma. To mourn is to feel the fullness of death, and to perceive the dying that live, and the life-takers.

What I have shared with you is my unique perspective of the history of colonialism, and in particular, its relation to the university. I have no intention of proving anything. If I set out to prove that things happened the way I perceive them, then I deny the validity of my intergenerational knowledge, which I have no desire to do. I seek only to mourn, to ontologize the bodies, to make sense of their deaths. My criterion is the convergence of ideas, nothing else.

I have become aware that the iteration in historiography creates divergent narratives of colonialism. It conceals our convergent experiences. While terror is a premise of colonialism, some of us feel it. Not because we are weak, it is because we have not yet been fully colonized. We mourn because we know what our ancestors lived, what we live, what has been lost. Decolonization requires that we acknowledge our shared experiences and that we collectively mourn, that we begin to see the strength in sadness. Decolonization begins when we perceive our collective grief.

WORKS CITED

Banaji, Jairus. (2013). "Putting Theory to Work". *Historical Materialism*, 21:4, 129-143.

Barthes, Roland. (1981). "The Discourse of History. In E.S. Shaffer (Ed.) *Comparative Criticism: A Yearbook.* Cambridge: Cambridge University Press, 7-20.

Belting, Hans. (2011). *Florence and Baghdad: Renaissance and Arab Science*. Cambridge: The Belnap Press of Harvard University Press.

Benjamin, Walter. (1968). *Illuminations*. New York: Schocken Books.

Bhabha, H. K. (2004). *The location of culture*. London ; New York: Routledge.

Bisman, Jayne E. (2012). "Budgeting for Famine in Tudor England, 1527-1528: social and policy perspectives". *Accounting History Review*, 22:2, 105-126.

Bradley, F.H. (1968). *The Presuppositions of a Critical History*. Don Mills: J.M. Dent & Sons Limited.

Bradshaw, David. (2004). *Aristotle East and West: Metaphysics and the Division of Christendom*. Cambridge: Cambridge University Press.

Burchardt, Jeremy F. S. (2000). "Land and Labour: Potato Grounds and Allotments in Nineteenth-Century Southern England". *Agricultural History*, 74:3, 667-684.

Byrd, J. A. (2011). *The transit of empire: Indigenous critiques of colonialism*. Minneapolis: University of Minnesota Press.

Charle, Christophe and Jacques Verger. (1994). *Histoire des universities*. Paris: Presses Universitaies de France.

Coope, Ursula. (2005). *Time for Aristotle: physics IV. 10-14*. Oxford: Clarendon.

Coulthard, Glen Sean. (2014). *Red Skin, White Masks: Rejecting the Colonial Politics of Recognition*. Minneapolis: University of Minneapolis Press.

Derrida, Jacques. (1993). *Specters of Marx: The State of Debt, the Work of Mourning and the New International*. New York: Routledge.

Dua and Lawrence. (2005). "Decolonizing Antiracism". Social Justice Vol. 32, No. 4,

Einstein, Albert. (2007). *Relativity: The Specific and General Theory*. East Bridgewater: Signature Press Editions.

Engels, Frederick. (1939). "Theoretical". *Anti-Duhring. Herr EugenDuhring's Revolution in Science*. International Publishers, 292-310.

Foster, John Bellamy. (2000). *Marx's Ecology: Materialism and Nature*. New York: Monthly Review Press.

Foucault, M. (1990). *The history of sexuality*. New York, NY: Vintage Books.

Franklin, Alfred. (1968). *La Sorbonne: Ses origins, saBibliothèque, les débuts de l'imprimerieà Paris et la Succession de Richelieu d'après des documents inèdits*. Amsterdam: Gérard Th. Van Heusen.

Fulda, Daniel. (2010). "Historicism as a Cultural Pattern: Practising a Mode of Thought". *Journal of the Philosophy of History*, 4, 138-153.

Furlong, John. (2013). *Education- An Anatomy of the Discipline: Rescuing the university project?* London: Routledge.

Goswami, Amit. (1993). "An idealist theory of ethics". *Creativity Research Journal*, 6:1-2, 185-196.

Green, V.H. (1974). *A History of Oxford University*. London: B.T. BatsfordLtsd.

Harvey, David.
-(2012). "History versus Theory: A Commentary on Marx's Method in *Capital*". *Historical Materialism*, 20:2, 3-38.
-(2001). *Spaces of capital: Towards a Critical Geography*. New York: Routledge.

Heckel, W., & Tritle, L. A. (2009). *Alexander the Great: A new history*. Chichester, U.K. ; Malden, MA: Wiley-Blackwell.

hooks, bell. (2013). *Writing Beyond Race: Living Theoy and Practice*. New York: Routledge.

Kelley, Donald R. (Ed.). (1997). *History and the Disciplines: The Reclassification of Knowledge in Early Modern Europe*. New York: The University of Rochester Press.

Levenson, Jonathan M. and J. David Sweatt. (2005). "Epigenetic Mechanisms in Memory Formation". *Nature Reviews*, 6, 108-118.

Lloyd, G.E.R.
-(2009). *Disciplines in the making: cross-cultural perspectives on elites, learning, and innovation*. Oxford: Oxford University Press.
-(1970). *Early Greek Science: Thales to Aristotle*. London: Chatto&Windus.

Lyons, Jonathan. (2009). *The House of Wisdom: How the Arabs Transformed Western Civilization*. New York: Bloomsbury Press.

MacKenzie, John M. (2008). "Irish, Scottish, Welsh and English Worlds? A Four-Nation Approach to the History of the British Empire". *History Compass*, 6:5, 1244-1263.

Marx, Karl. *Capital, Volume 1*. London: Penguin Books.

Matthen, Mohan.
- (2015). *The Oxford handbook of the philosophy of perception* (First edition.). Oxford University Press.
-(2005). *Seeing, doing, and knowing: A philosophical theory of sense perception*. Oxford ; New York: Oxford University Press.

McClellan, James E. III. (2010). *Colonialism and Science: Saint Domingue in the Old Regime*. Chicago: The University of Chicago Press.

McClellan, J. E. 1., &Regourd, F. (2011). *The colonial machine: French science and overseas expansion in the old regime*. Brepols.

Momigliano, A. (1966). Time in Ancient Historiography. *History and Theory,6*, 1-23.

Mukerji, Chandra. (2007). "Dominion, Demonstratio, and Domination: Religious Doctrine, Territorial Politics, and French Plant Collection". In Linda Schiebinger and Claudia Swan (Eds.) *Colonial Botany: Science, Commerce, and Politics in the Early Modern Period*. Philadelphia: University of Philadelpohia Press, 19-33.

Quijano, Anibal. (2007). "Questioning 'Race'"". *Socialism and Democracy*. 21:1, 45-53.

Rosemount, Franklin. (2009, July 7). "Karl Marx and the Iroquois". Retrieved from https://libcom.org/library/karl-marx-iroquois-franklin-rosemont

Rüegg, Walter. (1992). *A History of the University in Europe, Volume 1: Universities in the Middle Ages*. Cambridge: Cambridge University Press.

Saliba, George. (2007). *Islamic Science and the Making of the European Renaissance*. Cambridge: MIT Press.

Said, E. W. (1979). *Orientalism* (1st Vintage Books ed.). New York, NY: Vintage Books.

Schiebinger, Linda and Claudia Swan. (2007). "Introduction". In Linda Schiebinger and Claudia Swan (Eds.) *Colonial Botany: Science, Commerce, and Politics in the Early Modern Period*. Philadelphia: University of Philadelpohia Press, 1-18.

Skillman, Gilbert L. (2013). "The Puzzle of Marx's 'Results': A Tale of Two Theories". *History of Political Economy*, 45:3, 475-504.

Soffer, Reba N. (1994). *Discipline and Power: The University, History, and the Making of an English Elite, 1870-1930*. Stanford: Stanford University Press.

Thomson, Helen. (2015). "Study of Holocaust survivors finds trauma passed on to children's genes". *The Guardian*. <www.theguardian.com/science/2015/aug/21/study-of-

holocaust-survivors-finds-trauma-passed-on-to-childrens-genes>

Thompson, EP. "Agenda for Radical history". *Making History: Writings on History and Culture*. New York: The New York Press, 358-364.

Tierney, Michael. (1942). "Aristotle and Alexander the Great". *Studies: Irish Quarterly Review*, 31:122, 221-228.

Trouillot, M. (1995). *Silencing the past: Power and the production of history*. Boston, Mass.: Beacon Press.

Whitt, Laurelyn. (2009). *Science, Colonialism, and Indigenous Peoples: The Cultural Politics of Law and Knowledge*. Cambridge: Cambridge University Press.

Womack, Craig S. (2008). "A Single Decade: Book-Length Native Literary Criticism". In Craig S. Womack, Daniel Heath and Christopher B. Teuton (Eds.) *Reasoning Together: The Native Critics Collective*. Norman: University of Oklahoma Press, 3-104.

Woodham Smith, C. (1962). *The great hunger: Ireland 1845-1849.* -- ([1st ed.]. --.). New York: Harper & Row.

---

[i] "scale" The Canadia Oxford Dictionary. Ed. Barber, Katherine. :Oxford University Press, 2004. Oxford Reference. 2005.

[ii] "logic".The Canadia Oxford Dictionary. Ed. Barber, Katherine. :Oxford University Press, 2004. Oxford Reference. 2005.

[iii] "colonialism". The Canadia Oxford Dictionary. Ed. Barber, Katherine. :Oxford University Press, 2004. Oxford Reference. 2005.

www.ingramcontent.com/pod-product-compliance
Lightning Source LLC
Chambersburg PA
CBHW022135080426
42734CB00006B/368